CLUB MOTOR RACING

Jim Gavin

B.T. Batsford Ltd.

London

First published 1977

ISBN 0 713 4 0893 6

Phototypeset by Trident Graphics Ltd.,
Reigate, Surrey
Printed by
J. W. Arrowsmith Ltd., Bristol
for the Publishers
B.T. Batsford Ltd.
4 Fitzhardinge Street
London. W1H 0AH

Acknowledgment

The author would like to thank the R.A.C. Motorsport Division for their help and for the use of their Rules and Circuit Maps; the many Motor Club Secretaries who gave of their time; and Susie Read for her help in putting it all together.

Contents

Contents

List of Illustrations

Circuit Maps

Foreword

Motor racing is not all Formula 1 and internationally known names such as James Hunt and Nicki Lauda. Every weekend during the now almost year-long racing season in Great Britain, dozens of smaller races up and down the country cater for hundreds of amateur racing drivers and thousands of spectators.

Many of the drivers aspire to greater things and use these amateur, or Club races as they are more commonly known, merely as a brief but necessary stepping stone in furthering their driving career, while others seek no goal other than a chance to race against their fellow competitors and to feel for a short time each weekend the thrill of driving flat out in a racing car.

There are classes for everyone. You can enter your normal road car, driving it, as some still do, to and from the circuit each weekend and merely unloading the picnic hamper and wife and kids before venturing on to the track; or you can buy (or build) a car purely for racing and take to the circuit on a trailer.

The category in which a driver finds himself is usually dictated by finance, ability or aspiration or a combination of all three. Often a driver will start out in, say, a saloon car and find that while it is tremendously competitive, there is still not the thrill for him of open-wheel racing; while others may find that the expense of the pure racing car is eating too great a hole in their pockets and may be quite happy to change to driving a saloon.

The intention of this book therefore, is to help the intending competitor to decide which class of racing he should choose; to help the already established competitor understand a little of the other formulae to which he might like to change; and to give the enthusiastic spectator a better understanding of what motor racing at Club level is all about.

Reasons for Racing

Different reasons for wanting to race . . . fun or ambition . . . mechanics . . . marshalling.

Before even beginning to consider which type or class of racing one should take up, it is important to analyse ones feelings so as to decide why you want to go racing in the first place. Once you've decided your main reasons then, and only then, should you begin to look at the different classes and determine where you can best channel your efforts.

It may be difficult to put into words your real reasons. You might not even know them yourself. It may be just a 'gut feeling' that motor racing is to be your raison d'etre and that nothing else will satisfy you but to be out on the track battling it out with the big-boys. If that's the case then, as you graduate through Club racing, take a long hard look at long distance racing either in sports cars or saloons, especially on the continent, as the majority of club races in Great Britain last only about nine or ten minutes.

It might help if we take a look at some of the reasons which prompt normally sane people to risk life and limb and their bank balance, week-end after week-end, in an endless drive to use more and more petrol, tyres, engine, suspension and body bits as well as an inexhaustible amount of time and effort for no material rewards other than the odd little silver cup.

The four main categories into which people who go Club racing fall are:

1. Those who do it for fun.
2. Those who take it more seriously, probably chasing

Championship points.

3. The aspiring professionals.
4. The occasional, once or twice a year man.

Probably the most popular reason of all for going Club racing is for the sheer fun of it. Winning is not of primary importance, the mere fact of competing is all. This is plenty reason enough to allow the maximum amount of enthusiasm and fun with the least amount of seriousness. The British are great 'club' people and the atmosphere at any of the events run by the better known clubs throughout the year is always bubbling with cheerful chatter about the relative qualities (or lack of them) of each group's driver, the state of their car and the merits of the beer in the bar.

The driver who races for fun will probably not race more than a dozen times in the season, yet he will always get the maximum amount of enjoyment from his racing. What matter that the car only went on three cylinders and he finished last, or that he spun off three times during the race or never even made the race at all as he broke the gearbox in practice. The important thing is enjoyment and who is to say there is not as much fun to be had discussing what might have been rather than what actually was, in the pub on the way home.

People have even been known to go motor racing just to impress the 'birds'. A noble ambition indeed but one to be wary of. Usually one of two things will happen. Either, and this is the more common, the 'bird(s)' in question will undoubtedly be impressed alright, but it will be by some chap who finished in front of you in the race, is much better looking and came in a Rolls Royce anyway; or, you will begin to enjoy your racing so much that you will become totally engrossed in it and forget about the girl altogether.

One small word of warning. By all means have fun but don't forget the basic safety precautions. It is all too easy to overlook some small item in the final check before going on to the track and, should you have an accident, fate is no respecter of whether you were racing for fun or seriously.

Remember too, that there are other, perhaps more serious competitors about. They may well be racing for championship points or intent on beating a rival to the chequered flag, so don't let your track manners suffer just because you're not taking it as seriously as them.

The serious Club driver is one who will approach each season knowing exactly which events he will be entering and in what type of car. He will almost certainly be entered for at least one or two Championships running throughout the season and possibly even more. Usually he will have no aspirations towards becoming World Champion in Formula 1 and will probably even avoid Formula 3, but he will derive tremendous satisfaction and enjoyment from his racing and he and his fellow competitors will provide some of the best and closest racing to be had anywhere in Europe.

While there are drivers of this calibre in both the single seater and sports car formulae, for some reason the majority of them are to be found in saloon cars. Why this should be is hard to say, perhaps saloon cars stand up to being banged about better than the others and therefore even after a full roll the driver can be back out again the following week-end; but whatever the reason, saloon car races are invariably oversubscribed and the sight of a full field of the larger capacity Group 1 class howling through Woodcote corner at the end of the first lap on the Club circuit at Silverstone, is a sight worth travelling many miles for.

For the more serious competitor time availability is an important consideration. Motor racing will take up not only almost all your weekends during the season, but in the off-season you will be re-building engines, gear-boxes and suspensions as well as up-dating the body to the new seasons specifications. Mind you, there is only a very short off-season nowadays and from the beginning of March right through until the end of December there are very few week-ends when racing can't be found somewhere around Great Britain.

But it is not at week-ends alone that you will be involved in your racing. Any damage sustained during a race or any modifications or servicing will have to be done during the week so as to leave the precious time at the track the following week-end free for practice and minor adjustments. You will need either an understanding boss who will let you take long lunch breaks while you drive round desperately trying to get cranks re-ground, brakes re-lined and valve seats cut before the end of the week, or a long suffering wife or friend who will do all these chores for you.

For the aspiring professional racing driver, and by professional I mean a driver whose aim is Formula 1, fame and fortune, and ultimately the world championship, Club racing is merely a necessary stepping stone. While sports cars and saloons may at times be quicker than some of the single seater formulae, it is on single seaters that the would-be professional will almost certainly concentrate right from the beginning.

His career will probably start with a series of lessons at one of the major racing driver schools in the Formula Ford cars which are now the standard training cars at all these schools. If he shows promise he may well be supported by the school, either with a car or a contribution towards costs during his first forays into the racing world. Having gained his National licence in Club racing he may very well try some Formula Ford racing on the continent, and with luck and application (always assuming of course that he has the ability) will quickly get his full licence and begin the battle to finish in one of the first three places at the major National and International meetings.

Having become established as a top class Formula Ford man, either in Formula Ford 1600 or the later Formula Ford 2000, the next step will be into a Formula 3 car and here the real battle for success and recognition will begin. It might be thought that the next step would be into Formula Atlantic or Formula 2, but Formula 3 has become so competitive in its own right that consistent displays of real speed, flair and ability, have gained more than one driver an invitation to a test drive for a full Formula 1 team.

A classic example of a Formula 3 man making the jump to Formula 1 took place at the Formula 3 supporting races for the 1976 Monaco Grand Prix. The Formula 3 event was divided up into two heats and a final, and a brilliant showing by the Italian Bruno Giacomelli, who won the first heat after leading for the entire 16 laps, led to March director Max Mosley signing him up on a Formula 1 contract even *before* he went on to win the final.

Finally there is the occasional driver who competes just a few times a year in selected events. Typical of these are the gentlemen in vintage or historic car racing who bring their precious and generally beautifully and lovingly restored machines out for an airing at vintage car meetings. While the racing might not always be as fast and furious as in the normal Club events, one can hardly blame the drivers for not wanting to place their rare machinery at too much risk. However, it is always a stirring sight to see these machines from the past performing on the circuits every now and again, rather than forever being shut up in some museum, and indeed some of them are not driven all that cautiously.

Some people like to drive three or four times a year just to keep their licences 'open', allowing them to compete in such events as the 750 Club organised annual Six Hour Relay race at Silverstone. This is a tremendous event and well worth competing at least once for a driver of almost any standard. It is an event designed purely with the competitor in mind, and hardly in any way directed at spectators. Ostensibly the idea is for teams of cars of almost any shape, size, capacity or vintage to compete against each other by taking a sash around the club circuit more times than any other team during the six hours of the race. But the real reason, as far as the author can see, is to have a really good time, to psyche and sabotage the opposition outrageously, and to encourage the flow of beer from the paddock bar which remains open the whole day. Well worthwhile.

These then are the four basic reasons why people go club racing. Of course there are exceptions, as for example, in the case of a driver who sets out to compete with, say, a Mini or a sports car and has no initial ambition to progress further, but as a result of consistently good performances and a growing desire to take his racing more seriously, finds he wants to graduate to faster and more demanding formula. He can look either at the faster saloon classes or, should his ambition reach higher still, Formula Ford and even Formula 3. There are really no limiting factors other than ones own talent, ambition and the depth of ones pocket.

Indeed there have been a number of drivers who got into racing by accident and who made quite a success of it too. Maybe they went along to a race meeting with a friend just to watch, or maybe they began as a machanic/helper and discovered while testing, or while having a one-off drive as a reward, that they were faster than the actual owner. Jim Clark was one such as this. He had no great desire at the beginning to be a racing driver, either at Club level or at International level, indeed at any level, but he found within himself a latent talent which once realised took him to World Championship heights and to being one of racing's greatest drivers.

Suppose you have a passion for racing cars but you don't particularly want to drive them. Perhaps you can't afford to or you haven't got the ability, but you want to be around them anyway and with people who do actually race. Or perhaps you've been a spectator long enough and want to be more involved. Well then, your course is crystal clear . . . you become an unpaid helper/mechanic. One thing is certain, if you have even the slightest amount of mechanical ability or in other words if you can tell a crankshaft from a flat tyre, and you want to get involved, you can be up to your elbows in sweat and spanners in no time at all.

How to get started? No problem. The next time there's a race meeting involving the type of car you are interested in, get along there first thing in the morning before the spectators start to drift in. You'll see chaps struggling to unload cars from trailers without proper ramps, other chaps trying to change all four wheels on their racer while the thing is balanced on one small jack at one end and on a tool box at the other, and more chaps going quietly grey as they look for someone to tow them around the Paddock for the umpteenth time so they can start the engine.

Have a careful look around until you spot someone looking particularly harrassed, preferably working by himself, then pitch in and help. Don't introduce yourself, or ask silly questions or observe such inanities such as 'Did you know your radiator's leaking?' In fact, don't say anything at all. Just be useful in whatever way you can without getting in the man's was; hand him spanners; move trays of hot dirty engine oil out of his way so he doesn't step backwards into them and, if you want to really make an impact, hand him half of one of your ham standwiches.

After about half an hour if you've been doing well, which will mean you're just as mucky as the chap who owns the car, you might have your presence acknowledged by a grunt or two. A little later, when he looks thoughtfully at you for a moment and says, while jerking his thumb vaguely in the direction of about fifty other would-be racing drivers scattered about the Paddock and all with their own problems; 'See if you can borrow a torque spanner from one of those chaps', you'll then know you're elected.

Of course, the ultimate accolade comes at the end of the day when he's just about to drive off, after you've finally managed to get the lights on his trailer working, and he says casually, 'Are you by any chance going to be at Ingleston next Sunday?'.

There is one other way that an interested by-stander can get more involved with racing without actually racing or even without having to work on the car, and that is to become a Marshall. You'll certainly be close to the cars and will see all the drivers in all the different formulae from a much more interesting point of view. In fact, just as in the case of the mechanic/helper, being a Marshall gives one an excellent view-point from which to study the many different and complicated types of racing, so as to build up a picture of whichever class one should aim for should you later decide to become a driver.

The British Motor Racing Marshalls Club Ltd., (B.M.R.M.C.), was founded in 1957 by a small group of enthusiasts to improve the standard of marshalling at racing circuits throughout the country. The club has now over 1000 members and as well as supplying trained marshalls for all types of motor sport, provides full on and off circuit training for novice and new members.

Members usually start off as Course marshalls, inspecting the track during racing, removing stones and mud and bits that might fall off cars and, in the event of an accident, pushing the damaged car out of the way and helping the driver to safety. A Course marshall will usually operate from one of the many marshall's posts around the circuit and will be directly responsible to the post's Observer.

Observers are the eyes and ears of the Clerk of the Course and will report to him any cases of dangerous driving, or potentially dangerous cars, by the field telephone or radio which links all marshall's posts to Race Control.

The job of Fire and Incident marshall as can be imagined, is one of the most important of all and a very high degree of skill and training is necessary before reaching this standard. Hopefully many races would go by before his skills would be called-on, but in a bad crash his actions during the first few seconds of any fire that might break out could well mean life or death to a driver.

Paddock marshalls have a generally pretty thankless job, getting, as they do, to the circuit first thing in the morning, long before even the first drivers arrive and staying until the last have left in the evening. Their responsibility is to see that transporters, racing cars, service vehicles and all the myriad cars and hospitality wagons of the trade representatives are parked neatly in their proper pre-designated places. They also chase-up drivers who are tardy in getting their cars on to the track for their races, try to keep spectators from under the mechanics feet, spend hours trying to locate the owners of cars left, locked of course, right in the middle of the only access road to the track, and all in all have a pretty hard time of it.

A Start Line Marshall's job usually combines two duties. First of all he will see that the cars, as they come onto the start-line grid are in their proper positions, relative to each other. Positions are, of course, based on practice times with the fastest cars being at the front and the slower towards the back. As the count-down towards the actual start progresses, he will help clear mechanics, girl-friends and hangers-on away from the cars, while keeping his eyes open for last minute panics, such as a reluctant engine.

Flag marshalls have the important job of signalling to drivers all manner of information while racing is in progress. There will be one flag marshall facing the on-coming cars, while a second faces the other direction to spot incidents which may happen just after the post. Different coloured flags tell the driver of oil on the track, accident ahead, the fact that some-one is trying to pass him and so on.

How to become a marshall? Contact the General Secretary of the B.M.R.M.C., Mr. Len Pullen, Lynwood, 10 Church Drive, North Harrow, Middlesex, and he will put you in touch with your nearest area secretary.

One last point; if you think that being a marshall is primarily a good way of getting to see motor racing close up for free, then think again. It's hard work requiring concentration and dedication, often in foul weahter, and for very little reward other than the satisfaction of a job well done. People will be depending on you, not least of all the drivers and there will be times when your actions might well make all the difference between an incident and a tragedy.

Getting Started

Getting started . . . paperwork . . . sponsorship and responsibilities.

Club racing in Great Britain is governed by the Motor Sports Council which was created in 1975, by the Royal Automobile Club. The rulings and decisions of the Motor Sport Council are implemented by the Motor Sport Division of the R.A.C. which operates from 31 Belgrave Square, London S.W.1. It is from Belgrave Square (usually known simply as 'The R.A.C.' or more colloquially as "Auntie"), that all legal requirements, rules and regulations and decisions regarding racing come. They have absolute power and create the Standing Supplementary Regulations under which events are run. They have the power to suspend or take away a competitor's licence to race and every now and again hold tribunals to examine cases of careless or dangerous driving on the track. An appearance at one of these tribunals is to be avoided like the plague.

The actual races are organised by individual motor clubs throughout the country who produce Additional Supplementary Regulations to go with the Standing Regulations already mentioned. The two biggest and most important clubs are the British Racing and Sports Car Club and the British Automobile Racing Club. Membership of either (or both) of these clubs will bring invitations to race at events organised, not just by the main club, but by almost every other club of any importance throughout the country.

The first requirement before going racing is to get a

Competition Licence. These come in three grades; Restricted, National and International. The National and International licences will come later and are granted upon your completion of a requisite number of lower grade races without any adverse reports from the official observers.

To qualify for a Restricted licence you must hold an ordinary Road Traffic Act driving licence (not provisional) and you must submit details of any physical disability you might have. When you get your licence you will be sent an R.A.C. medical card which must be filled in by your G.P. Take this with you to all events in which you're driving, you may be asked to show it. The application form for a Restricted licence is available from the R.A.C. and the licence has to be renewed each year.

With your licence you will get a copy of the R.A.C. Motor Sport Year Book, usually known, more affectionately, as the 'Blue Book'. This gives a list of events for the year, the names and addresses of all the R.A.C. affiliated clubs around the country, specifications of all the recognised formulae, regulations for various championships, and so on.

You might also ask the R.A.C. for a copy of their annual Motor Sport Regulations. This contains details of General Competition Rules, Standing Supplementary Regulations, vehicle regulations, medical requirements, insurance details and dozens of other snippets of information worth knowing. While you're putting together your little library you might consider investing in what the author considers to be two of the finest books ever written for the aspiring racing driver: *The Racing Driver: the Theory and Practice of Fast Driving* by Denis Jenkinson, and *The Technique of Motor Racing* by Piero Taruffi. You might have to scratch around a bit to get them but they are a mine of information for anyone interested in driving as an art.

To be up-graded from Restricted status to National, you must compete in at least six races at no less than two different circuits. At each of these events you should hand in your licence to the R.A.C. Steward at race control before racing starts, and, if you drive properly and don't do a naughty, he will sign it for you before you leave. It might not be absolutely necessary to actually finish a race to get a signature.

During the six races you will be required to carry on the back of your car a black cross with 6-in long arms on a yellow ground 7-in square. Inch-wide black tape will do splendidly for the cross. Having carried this like a leper's bell for your six events you can get rid of the cross but you must keep the square until the National licence is actually in your possession.

To get a full International licence you must, in addition to getting your National licence, finish in two more National races, or one National and two restricted or four Restricted; again without adverse reports.

Up to the end of the 1960s advertising was not allowed on racing cars in any shape or form. Not even a tiny 'Champion' or 'Castrol' sticker. Not quite the thing, you know. Anyway, the R.A.C. relented and soon cars began carrying all manner of stickers and devices until in a very short time not only were cars being covered with the names of motor trade suppliers, but some became mobile bill-boards for all manner of goodies from cigarettes, toothpaste and boutiques, through art galleries, fork-lift trucks and paint and on to cups of sugar, cheese, underwear and rubber goods. A new word swept through the racing world like wildfire and soon the great chase was on. Sponsorship. That was the thing; someone else to pick up all the bills in return for his name on the side of your car, while you carried on racing and cheerfully spending the unfortunate gentleman's money on engines, gearboxes, replacement body panels et al. But it couldn't last, and inevitably deals began to go sour.

Of course there were professional teams who worked out proper contracts and deals between sponsors and themselves but these by definition tended to be not strictly 'Club' teams, but teams already at or near the top in Formulas 1, 2 or 3; or passing through Club racing as a stepping stone to the top and acting in a professional and business-like way, not just towards their racing but to allied interests. It was mainly with the more amateur partnerships that the majority of misunderstanding and disillusionment arose, but this was not always just the fault of the driver, and inevitably there were faults on both sides. In many cases these faults still exist today.

The usual reaction from a sponsor who had given, say, £500 to a racing driver in return for having his name on the car, was: 'Well, I gave this guy £500 and he said that not only would my name be on his car, but he had a good chance of winning races and that would mean pictures of the car would be in the paper and in the magazines. He also said that quite a few of the races would be televised and that television had an audience of seven million' etc. etc. Exit one sponsor. As for the driver; at the beginning of the season when all was sunshine, smiles and handshakes, freed from money problems for a while he concentrated on his racing with his own personal aims in view (be it a particular Championship, or just winning his class against guys who had previously beaten him), and gave not a further thought to the man who was in effect buying him further racing opportunities.

Before even approaching a sponsor, a driver MUST work out what he has to offer. A name on the side of a car is just not enough; in fact nowadays, with not just the cars but drivers overalls and even their crash helmets plastered with advertising, one new name will hardly even be noticed.

What a driver can offer however is a basis around which the sponsor can base *his* advertising/public relations. If the sponsor owns a garage then perhaps he might think of having three or four 'open' evenings a year, perhaps when a new model is announced, or when he is having a free 'Check-up' week. The open evening would be held in his showroom for invited guests who would be given coffee and biscuits (or drinks if he can afford it), and they could each be given a leaflet describing the garage and how it is the best in the area and how he, the proprietor, always has their best interests at heart. The leaflet would be accompanied by brochures on whatever latest car might be on offer, but the main attraction of the evening would be our friend's racing car, set on blocks so people didn't have to bend over too much to look into it. Our friendly driver would also be present, smartly dressed and NOT drinking, answering questions about racing and gently praising his sponsor and his sponsor's products.

The driver should also ensure that the garage staff feel that the car is 'their' car and he should keep them fully informed about his intended racing programme, results and whatever went wrong. A mechanic in an ordinary garage, working on ordinary cars all day and everyday, will invariably be secretly pleased and proud that 'his' car is racing at so-and-so circuit. This will bring a lot of good feelings both on the workshop floor and in the sales office and it will all be reflected back on the sponsor.

Suppose the sponsor doesn't own a garage. Say, he runs a chain of shops. Well then, periodically throughout the year he might want to impress particular clients or buyers. Why not suggest that instead of giving them a smart lunch or dinner that he takes them to the races to see 'his' car. On that particular day for heavens sake don't be in dirty overalls. Have both the car and yourself and any helpers you might have looking really smart. Your finishing position in the race is not the most important thing that day. When the sponsor appears give him and his colleagues your complete attention. Remember he is not an interruption of your work, he is a good part of the reason for it. When you've explained all about 'their' car and its chances in the race and the opposition it's up against, take them for a conducted tour of the Paddock. Don't make them walk too far or for too long otherwise they will just get bored. Have a short route worked out beforehand taking in particular cars of interest which they might have read or heard about even though they know nothing about racing. If you happen to know a particularly famous driver imagine how pleased your party will be if they are introduced.

There are many other things you can do which will only take a little thought. Why not give each of the circuit visitors a good 10in x 8in photograph of the car with the sponsor's name well to the fore. Have them framed so they are hung on a wall and not shoved away in a drawer. Point out to your sponsor that the catering facilities at circuits are usually pretty bad and suggest that he bring along a hamper lunch. Don't forget to join the visitors for lunch. If between you you can manage to get a caravan along to the circuit, so much the better.

The main point in all this is that the driver must devote a certain amount of his time to cultivating his sponsor right through the whole season. Write him a short report after each meeting telling him about everything that happened whether good or bad. You will naturally be keeping a similar report but in much more detailed form for your own records, so that when you visit that particular circuit again you will have data on previous lap times, tyres, condition of track etc.

Keep a detailed account of all your expenses. It will be no surprise to you how the bills mount up but it will be refreshing to your sponsor at the end of the season to see that his money was all spent on the car and not on booze and 'birds'. It should also help you in your efforts to get a little more money from him the following year.

Sponsorship of a driver carries with it a responsibility every bit as great as that of the driver towards the sponsor. A sponsorship deal must be worked at by both partners if it is to be a success and if the sponsor does not know this and imagines that when he hands over his money his duties are finished and all he has to do is sit back and wait for the rewards to come rolling in, then he is very much mistaken.

It may not be generally known, but in the majority of the

bigger and well known sponsorship deals the sponsor may be expected to spend around the same amount of money in promoting his advertising/public relations interests in a car or cars as he has spent on the actual racing. If, for example, £50,000 has been given to a team to run a certain number of events then the sponsor will expect to spend another £50,000 or thereabouts on promotions involving his product with the team and with motor racing. It's a sobering thought, but one which should be remembered by both sides.

Of course figures like these will never be reached in Club racing (will they?) but the proportions will not be that much different. Suppose a sponsor agrees to pay £1,000 towards the cost of a year's racing in a championship involving around twenty races. If he is to get his money's worth he will have to be prepared to spend another £1,000 on promoting his product through the image he has created by being involved in motor racing. Should the total budget he can afford to spend only come to £1,000 then the sharing will have to be £500 to the racing and £500 on promotion. Should his driver try to persuade him otherwise, then he is doing both his sponsor and motor racing a disservice. Sponsorship must always first and foremost be based on a proper and perfectly understood business relationship between the sponsor and the driver. It is not a carte blanche to spend another's money and a driver should *never* approach a sponsor until he has worked out a carefully prepared proposition whereby the sponsor can reasonably expect to get back from his motor racing involvement as good a return (or close to it) as he might expect from any other form of investment.

In a situation where a sponsor fully appreciates that he is spending more on his involvement than he can ever hope to regain in monetary terms, then it is not sponsorship but patronage. And patrons, sadly, are a dying breed. A good patron must be the greatest gift known to man, to any young racing driver, but they are awfully hard to find. If you do have the good luck to find one (he will probably find you) and get adopted, then cherish him.

For your first few races it is highly unlikely that you will have anyone sponsoring you and you will be entering the car under your own name. In this case you will only be allowed to have your own name and your mechanics name displayed on the car. If you get a sponsor you will need a Trade Licence from the R.A.C. before his name can be added but you can also add on up to eight pairs of other stickers. A Trade Licence costs £25 at the time of writing. Should you want to go even further you will need an Open Trade Licence which entitles you to write just about anything at all on the car as long as it's not too offensive. This last licence will cost a mighty £85.

Comparative Performances

Racing speeds . . . lap records . . . race winners . . . Class winners . . . differences between Formulae . . . list of comparative lap records . . . list of successful winners . . . buying a car . . . new or second-hand.

Speed comparison

Sheer flat out speed is seldom as important in a racing car as all-round performance. This all-round performance is a combination of acceleration, braking, cornering power, ease of handling and "chuckability" and is best expressed in lap times round a racing circuit.

Each different formula and class of racing has its lap record to aim at and while records will be broken as cars and circuits improve year after year, comparisons will still be valid and will be of interest to anyone concerned with the relative track performances of the many different categories of racing available to the Club driver.

At the end of each racing season *Autoport* publishes a Lap Records Survey of all British circuits by journalist Mike Kettlewell, giving driver, car type, time and speed for each class of racing together with the date on which the record was set. This runs to twelve large pages packed with information and in it there are many names, some famous such as Nicki Lauda whom you might expect to find, but others whose records have stood for a remarkably long time and whose names are now only remembered by afficionados. Archie Scott-Brown's Formula 1 record for example, set in a Connaught Alta around the Brands Hatch Club circuit still stands twenty years later.

So you see, there are plenty of challenges still to be met and in the enormous number of different classes available there will always be a place in the record books for the aspiring Club driver, whatever his ability, ambitions and depth of pocket. Remember too that the lap record list shown at the end of this section only covers the short circuit at just one track, Brands Hatch. There are some 22 different circuit configurations in total, on 16 different tracks around the country, so there's lots of room for everyone.

Also at the end of this section there is a breakdown of Club race winners of 1975. This too is taken from *Autosport's* annual analysis of season long-race winners and is a fascinating list which should be studied in conjunction with the list of lap records. The list of race winners is interesting not only to see which drivers were most successful but, more important to the newcomer, to see which cars were winning. One can also see the breakdown of Class and Outright wins in relation to the total number of wins.

In Formula Ford races for instance (either FF1600 or FF2000), there is, in effect, only one class. That means that in a Formula Ford race with, say, twenty starters there will be prizes for 1st, 2nd and 3rd places awarded and that, apart from any Championship points which might be going for lower places, will be all. So in the unlikely event of all twenty starters finishing, three would get awards and seventeen would get nothing.

By contrast, in a Modsports (Modified Sportscars) race there are four classes: (a) up to 1150cc; (b) 1150cc to 1500cc; (c) 1500cc to 2000cc and (d) over 2000cc. So it can be seen that in a Modsports race of twenty cars, as well as overall placings of 1st, 2nd and 3rd, there will be Class placings down to three places with the result that almost everyone that manages to finish has a good chance of getting some sort of prize.

The same thing happens with lap records. Again in Modsports you will only be competing for a record lap against perhaps five or six others in your own Class, instead of against the whole field.

All this is relevant to any aspiring Club racer. The true sportsman, or so one is led to believe, competes for the pleasure of competing, but it is rare to see a driver express displeasure at winning or receiving a silver cup.

It is of course quite possible to win a season-long Championship without ever actually winning a single race outright. This has happened quite often, notably to Tony Lanfranchi, that doyen of Club drivers, with his Russian built Moskvich in 1973. The car was a consistent winner in its price class in Production Saloon racing and even though it ran way behind the race leaders, it amassed enough points to win the overall Championship outright.

There are other points to be considered when comparing speeds and formulae. For instance the amount of engine tuning permitted, what sort of tyres are used and with what rim width restrictions; what modifications are allowed to suspension and bodywork; the use of lightweight panels and the age of the car; all of these vary from formula to formula. In Clubmans racing the two different classes have two different engine types although the upper capacity limit is the same in both cases. In Class A there are virtually no restrictions on modifications and even superchargers and turbo-chargers are allowed, whereas Class B is restricted (?) to engines complying to the Formula Ford 1600 specification.

In Modified Sportscars considerable modifications, as the name of the formula suggests, are allowed and the different Classes are divided up by engine capacity; yet in Production Sportscars the cars are kept as near standard as possible consistent with safety and the Classes are determined by price. Modsports cars use racing tyres and Prodsports use road tyres. Formula Ford originally used road tyres but now uses racing tyres of specified type and size. So comparisons have to be made with care and with the knowledge of all the modifications and alterations allowed under the myriad regulations and rules.

Apart from out and out pure racing cars, Clubmans Class A cars are really fast and for sheer speed would be hard to beat if that is what you are really looking for. Super Vee, perhaps surprisingly, is faster than Formula Ford, and also notably fast is the Vauxhall Firenza which Gerry Marshall has driven in the Super Saloon Class around Brands Hatch Club circuit in less than the almost magic 50-second barrier.

Amongst the slowest cars are the historic examples, but this is almost certainly due to their owners reluctance to risk damage by driving them at racing speeds. The standard saloon classes are also pretty slow but what may be lacking in sheer speed will usually be compensated for in excitement with identical performances between the cars giving very close racing. Also, the historic cars while they may not be driven all that fast, have enormous spectator appeal and their monetary values are fast climbing.

Personal fitness, reaction time and courage can also influence the choice of a car or formula. A single seater or Clubmans car will be very fast and will need really quick reactions to be driven to its full potential, but will repay the effort by giving a great impression of speed with the drivers bottom an inch and a half above the tarmac, his eyes looking between the front wheels, and his goggles and helmet constantly buffeted by the elements. Saloon cars on the other hand give better protection from the weather or in the event of an accident, and on the whole are easier and less demanding to drive, particularly in the slower classes.

If you are at all undecided about which Class of racing to choose, then do not make a hasty decision just to get out on the track quickly. Study the subject carefully until you are quite sure that you know what you want to do and which car you should buy. Make a short-list of formulae which appeal to you; have a look in the classified advertisements in *Autosport* for several weeks to get an idea of prices; study the lists of race winners as reported in the motoring magazines to see whether they are really amateurs against whom you might stand some sort of a chance, or whether they are Works supported, either officially or unoffically. Production Saloon racing for example looks exciting and on the surface it looks as though a determined privateer should be able to mix it with the race leaders, but invariably they have huge budgets behind them and even the entries in the slower Classes are almost all backed by whichever importer or manufacturer enters them.

When you've finally decided which type or class of racing on which to concentrate, there will be the question of choosing the actual car. Unless you intend competing in one of the comparatively cheaper formula such as Mini 7 or 750, you probably won't try building your own, at least not in the beginning, so your first decision will be to buy new or second-hand. As this will almost certainly depend on the size of your bank balance, this decision, at least, won't take too long to make.

Should you decide to buy second-hand, think carefully before making a choice. If you intend racing purely for fun then you need not necessarily spend too much money on a car as you and your friends will probably get as much enjoyment out of trying to get the blessed thing running in the paddock as you would if you were out on the track; but on the other hand, if you intend to take your racing more seriously, a lot more care will have to be taken, since no matter how good a driver you are, sheer driving ability will never get you up with the front runners if you have a bad car.

Analysing the results of races during the season to see which cars are winning is probably as good a way as any to help in deciding which model to buy, and asking around the paddock at race meetings or looking in the classified pages of *Autosport* should flush out some suitable examples in your price range. As far as vetting the car is concerned if you're not sure about doing it yourself, you could take along an aquaintance such as a mechanic who has worked on the particular type or, better still, have the owner take it round your nearest racing circuit on a general practice day.

If he can manage to lap at, or near, his claimed times for the car then that's at least an indication that there can't be too much wrong with it. Be sure to bring the money with you to the circuit though, as you will not want him doing anything silly to the car like taking it home to give it 'a good check-up' before you get it, and inadvertantly swopping the engine for a worn out practice unit.

Should you be in the lucky position of being able to afford a new car, there is a list at the back of this book of the major British manufacturers of specialised racing cars who will be only too delighted to relieve you of your money. Generally cars are supplied in 'rolling-chassis' form. That is to say without an engine and sometimes even without a gearbox. But most of the manufacturers will suggest a particular engine builder of their choice and will probably arrange for the engine to be fitted at their works. Once again, an analysis of results throughout the season will give an indication of which engine to buy as obviously the car/engine combination which does most of the winning will be your first choice.

Finally, some firms actually operate a racing car hire scheme, but as this idea would not seem to have any degree of permanence your best bet, should you decide to hire cars rather than buy them, would again be to look in the classified pages of the enthusiast magazines.

BRANDS HATCH LAP RECORDS 1975

Class	Car	Time Secs	Speed mph
Outright	5000 March	43.7	102.15
Atlantic	Modus 1600cc	44.0	101.45
Formula Ford 2000	Various	49.0	91.10
Formula Ford 1600	Various	51.4	86.85
Formula Super Vee	Supernova	48.2	92.61
Formula Vee	Austro Vee	58.8	82.97
Formula 4	Delta	51.0	87.52
Monoposto	Brabham	50.6	88.22
Libre	March	44.4	100.54
Sports GT to 1300cc	Alexis	51.6	86.51
Sports GT 1300–1650cc	Astra	49.8	89.60
Sports GT over 1650cc	March	48.0	93.00
Clubmans full race	U2	46.6	95.79
Clubmans Formula Ford engines	Gryphon	50.4	88.57
750	DNC	57.4	77.77
1300	Navajo	52.4	85.19
Modified Sports to 1150cc	Davrian	54.0	82.68
Modified Sports 1150–2000cc	Elan	52.2	85.51
Modified Sports 2001–3000cc	Porsche 911	51.6	86.51
Modifed Sports over 3000	XK120	52.0	85.84
Production Sports £1400–£2250	MGB/Morgan	63.6	70.19
Production Sports £2250–£4000	Europa	59.8	74.65
Special Saloons to 850cc	Imp	55.6	80.29
Special Saloons to 851–1000cc	Imp	52.8	84.55
Special Saloons 1001–1300cc	Mini	53.0	84.23
Special Saloons over 1300cc	Firenza	49.2	90.73
Mini Seven 848cc	Mini	61.0	73.18
Mini Miglia 998cc	Mini	57.6	77.50
Group 1 to 1600cc	Toyota	57.4	77.77
1601–2500cc	Mazda/Escort	56.2	79.43
2501–4000cc	Capri	56.2	79.43
over 4000cc	Camaro	54.2	82.36

Class	Car	Time Secs	Speed mph
Standard Production			
Saloons to £1299	Imp	64.6	69.10
£1300–£1699	Mazda	61.4	72.70
£1700–£2299	Capri	61.6	72.47
over £2300	Camaro	58.6	76.18
Escort Championship	Mexico	61.6	72.47
Renault R5 Championship	R5	70.2	63.59
Historic post-war racing cars	Connaught	71.8	62.17
Historic pre-war racing cars	Alfa Romeo	62.4	71.54
Historic Sports Cars to 2000cc	Lotus 11	57.8	77.23
Historic Sports Cars over 2000cc	Lister Jaguar	58.4	76.44
Thoroughbred Sports			
Cars to 1650cc	MGA	74.0	60.32
1651–2700cc	Morgan+4	63.8	69.97
over 2700cc	Aston-Martin	63.8	69.97
Classic Saloon			
Cars to 1200cc	A35	69.8	63.95
1201–1900cc	Borgward	67.4	66.23
1901–2700cc	Zephyr 2	66.4	67.23
over 2700cc	Jaguar 7/9	71.4	62.52

The following list shows the winners during the 1975 season, and, if studied in conjunction with the section on Lap Speeds, should help in deciding which formula will suit you best,

CLUB RACE WINNERS

			Out-right	Class	Total
1.	Geoff Lees	1.6 FF Royale-Minister RP21	32	—	32
2.	John Homewood	1.0 Sunbeam Imp/5.3 Vauxhall Magnum-Aston Martin V8	21	10 (9)	31 (30)
3.	Gerry Marshall	2.3 Vauxhall Magnum Coupé/2.3 & 2.5 Vauxhall Firenza t/c/5.0 Vauxhall Firenza-Repco V8/2.0 Triumph Dolomite Sprint/2.5 Ford Zephyr 6 Mk 2	23	7	30
4.	Jock Robertson	2.0 Mazda RX3 Coupé	17	11	28
5.	Nick Whiting	2.0 Ford Escort FVC	24	—	24
6.	Geoff Friswell	1.6 Mallock U2-Hart Mk 16/1.6 Mallock U2-Davron Mk 11B/14	22	1 (—)	23 (22)
7.	Kenny Gray	1.6 FF Van Diemen-Scholar RF75	20	—	20
8.	Peter Baldwin	1.3 Mini-Clubman BDA	3	17	20
9.	Kenny Allen	1.0 Clan Crusader-Imp	5	15 (14)	20 (19)
=10.	Nick Adams	1.6 FF Mallock U2-Close/Holbay Mk 14/1.6 Mallock/U2-Close Mk 17	3	16	19
=10.	Phil Winter	1.3 Mini-Cooper S	3	16	19
12.	Tiff Needell	1.6 FF Elden-Scholar PH10C/1.6 FF Crosslé-Scolar 25F/2.0 FF Hawke-Holbay DL14	17	—	17
13.	Chris Meek	1.6 Lotus Europa Special	14	3 (2)	17 (16)
14.	Graham Wennham	848 Mini	15	1	16
15.	Roger Gill	850 Hillman Imp	1	15	16
16.	Chris Alford	1.6 Morgan 4/4	—	15	15
17.	Willie Green	3.8 Jaguar E Lightweight/2.5 Maserati 250F/3.3 Ferrari 275LM	13	2 (1)	15 (14)
18.	Jim Walsh	1.6 FF Hawke-Scholar DL12/1.6 FF Hawke-Close DL12	14	—	14
19.	Jeff Ward	1.0 Hillman Imp	9	5	14
20.	Phil Dowsett	3.0 Ford Capri 3000GT/1.6 FF Crosslé-Minister 25F	2	12	14
21.	David Enderby	850 Mini	—	14	14
22.	Andrew Smith	1.6 Lotus Elan	8	6 (4)	14 (12)
23.	Robin Gray	3.5 Morgan Plus 8	5	8 (5)	13 (10)
24.	Derek Daly	1.6 FF Crosslé-Minister 30F	12	—	12
=25.	Andy Barton	1.6 Lotus-BDA 69/1.6 March-BDA 73B	11	1	12
=25.	John Brindley	5.7 Chevrolet Camaro Z28/2.0 Mazda RX3 Coupé	11	1	12
=28.	Eric Smith	1.3 Mini-Clubman BDA	3	9	12
=28.	Iain McLaren	2.0 Chevron-Hart B26/31 BDG	11	—	11
=28.	Kim Perry	742 DNC-Reliant Mk 3	11	—	11
30.	Ian Forrest	1.0 Hillman Imp	3	8	11
=32.	Ian Flux	FV Scarab Mk 1	10	—	10
32.	Eddie Jordan	1.6 FF Crosslé-Woodie 30F	10	—	10
=32.	Neil McGrath	1.0 Renault 5TL/1.6 Ford Escort Mexico	10	—	10
=32.	Brian Rice	5.7 Chevrolet Camaro Z28	10	—	10
=32.	Fergus Tait	1.0 Delta-Delta/Ford 1RF4	10	—	10
=32.	John Wingfield	1.8 Brabham-Somers/FVC BT35	10	—	10
38.	Richard Jenvey	1.6 Lotus Elan/2.0 Vogue-Ark/BDG SP	9	1	10

			Out-right	Class	Total
=39.	Simon Packford	1.0 Davrian-Imp Mk 7	3	7	10
=39.	Derek Walker	1.0 Fiat 850 Coupé-Ford	3	7	10
=41.	Ivan Dutton	3.0 Ford Capri 3000GT/1.3 Simca Rallye 1	—	10	10
=41.	Tony Stubbs	1.2 Lada 1200	—	10	10
=43.	Bob Davies	1.3 Davis-Ford Mk 1	9	—	9
=43.	Rad Dougall	1.6 FF Royale-Scholar RP21	9	—	9
=43.	Norman Hodgson	1.8 Ford Escort FVC	9	—	9
=43.	Rick Morris	1.6 FF Hawke-Scholar DL12	9	—	9
=43.	Patsy McGarrity	1.6 Chevron-BDA B29	9	—	9
=43.	Gunnar Nilsson	F3 March-Novamotor/Toyota 753/1.6 Chevron-Swindon B29 BDA	9	—	9
=43.	Steve Thompson	1.6 Ford Escort Mexico	9	—	9
49.	Alan Curnow	1.0 Mini	8	1	9
=50.	Brian Murphy	4.4 Jaguar E	7	2	9
=50.	Frank Sytner	1.6 Mallock U2-Davron Mk 118/16/ 3.8 Jaguar E Lightweight/1.9 Mallock U2-Hart Mk 17 BDG	7	2	9
52.	Simon Phillips	2.0 Fraser Nash Le Mans Replica/ 2.0 Cooper-Bristol Mk 2/2.0 BMW 328	2	7	9
=53.	Alex Ferrada	1.6 FF Mallock U2-Davron Mk 16	—	9	9
=53.	John Kirk	1.1 Davrian-Imp Mk 5	—	9	9
55.	David Ham	3.8 Lister-Jaguar	5	4 (3)	9 (8)
56.	John Cooper	5.0 Ford GT40/2.8 Porsche Carrera RSR	3	6 (5)	9 (8)
57.	Reg Woodcock	2.2 Triumph TR3	—	9 (8)	9 (8)
=58.	Matthew Argenti	1.6 FF Van Diemen-Scholar RF75	8	—	8
=58.	Mike Blanchet	1.6 FF Crosslé-Minister 30F/1.6 FF Lotus-Minister 61	8	—	8
=58.	Mike Nugent	1.8 Lotus Elan 26R	8	—	8
62.	Eddie Labinjoh	1.1 Fisher-BL Spyder/2.0 Alfa Romeo 2000GTV	7	1	8
63.	Richard Thwaites	2.0 Elva-BMW Mk 7S	4	4	8
64.	Stee Griffin	1.4 Mini-Cooper S	3	5	8
65.	Gerald Clark	1.3 Mini-Cooper S	1	7	8
=66.	Simon Watson	0.9 Sunbeam Imp Sport	—	8	8
=66.	Terry Grimwood	1.5 MG Midget	—	8	8
68.	Dave Bettinson	1.6 Lotus-Holbay 7	4	4 (3)	8 (7)
69.	Ian McCullough	1.3 Austin-Healey Sprite	1	7 (6)	8 (7)
70.	Ken Shipley	1.6 FF Mallock U2-Rowland Mk 11B	—	8 (7)	8 (7)
=71.	John Allan	1.2 Allan-Ford Mk 4	7	—	7
=71.	Joe Applegarth	1.6 Brabham-Ford BT2 3C	7	—	7
=71.	Ian Briggs	1.0 March-Felday/MAE 733/1.0 Mini	7	—	7
=71.	Jim Evans	2.0 Ford Escort RS2000 Turbo	7	—	7
=71.	David Kennedy	1.6 FF Crosslé 30F	7	—	7
=71.	David Orbell	1.6 Mallock U2-Holbay Mk 11B/16	7	—	7
=71.	John Simpson	1.6 FF Nike-Scholar Mk 10	7	—	7
=71.	Mick Starkey	1.6 FF Merlyn-Scholar Mk 20A	7	—	7
=71.	Brian Whiting	1.9 Ford Escort BDE	7	—	7
80.	John Evans	1.8 Lotus Elan	6	1	7
81.	John Pearson	3.8 Jaguar XK120	4	3	7
82.	Keith Ashby	1.3 MG Midget	3	4	7
=83.	Jim Adamson	1.0 Davrian-Imp Mk 7	1	6	7
=83.	Ian Smith	2.0 Mazda RX3 Coupé	1	6	7
85.	John Morgan	3.8 Jaguar Mk 1	5	2 (1)	7 (6)
86.	Tony Allies	1.3 Mini-Clubman	1	6 (5)	7 (6)
87.	Ian Hall	1.1 Mini-Jem Mk 2	—	7 (6)	7 (6)
=88.	Derrick Brunt	5.7 Chevrolet Camaro Z28/3.0 BMW Si	5	2 (—)	7 (5)
=88.	Barry Reece	850 Mini	—	7 (4)	7 (4)
=89.	Tony Dean	5.0 Chevron-Morand/Chevrolet B24/28	6	—	6
=89.	Bernard Devaney	1.6 FF Hawke Rowland DL12	6	—	6
=89.	Ray Edge	1.6 Mallock U2-Davron/Holbay Mk 14/17	6	—	6
=89.	John Gale	1.3 MG Midget	6	—	6

			Out-right	Class	Total
=89.	Derek Lawrence	2.0 FF Crosslé-Titan 31F	6	—	6
=89.	Stu. Lawson	=89. 1.6 FF Hawke-Scholar DL12	6	—	6
=89.	John Morrison	FSV Supernova- Heidegger BH5/FSV Supernova-Daghorn BH4	6	—	6
=89.	David MacPherson	1.6 FF Dulon-Minister MP17	6	—	6
=89.	Paul Sleeman	1.6 FF Merlyn-Minister Mk 11A	6	—	6
=89.	Tony Strawson	4.7 Ford Capri V8/7.2 Ford Capri-Chevrolet V8	6	—	6
=89.	Mike Young	FSV Modus-Heidegger M2	6	—	6
=100.	Glenn Eagling	1.6 FF Van Diemen-Scholar RF75	5	1	6
=100.	John Bright	1.6 FF Merlyn-Whitehurst Mk 11/1.6 FF Royale-Whitehurst RP21	5	1	6
102.	John Fyda	1.0 Hillman Imp	4	2	6
103.	Graham Goode	1.3 Ford Escort BDA	2	4	6
104.	Peter Cartlidge	1.0 Austin A40-Ford	1	5	6
105.	John Webb	1.6 Lotus Elan 26	—	6	6
106.	Andy Houston	1.6 FF Gryphon-Lion C4A	—	6 (5)	6 (5)
=108.	Creighton Brown	1.6 Mallock U2-Close Mk 17	5	—	5
=108.	Arthur Collier	5.0 Skoda-Chevrolet S110R V8	5	—	5
=108.	Russell Dell	1.0 Mini	5	—	5
=108.	Bill Dryden	2.5 Vauxhall-Firenza t/c	5	—	5
=108.	Tim Green	742 Time Reliant Mk 3	5	—	5
=108.	Philip Guerola	1.8 Brabham-Norvic/FVC BT30	5	—	5
=108.	Rob Haigh	1.9 MGA	5	—	5
=108.	Kelvin Hesketh	1.6 FF Crosslé-Minister 30F	5	—	5
=108.	David Kemp	1.6 FF Merlyn-Abbot Mk 20A	5	—	5
=108.	Paul Rhodes	1.8 Ford Escort FVC	5	—	5
=108.	Terry Richards	1.6 FF Merlyn-Rowland Mk 11A	5	—	5
=108.	Bernard Vermilio	1.6 FF Merlyn-Scholar Mk 29/2.0 FF Merlyn-Scholar Mk 28	5	—	5
=108.	Rob Wicken	1.6 FF Merlyn- Minister Mk 17A	5	—	5
=121.	Gerry Brown	1.5 MG TC	4	1	5
=121.	Nick Faure	3.0 Porsche Carrera RS	4	1	5
123.	Derek Shortall	1.6 Gryphon-Ford C4A	3	2	5
=124.	Gerry Glass	850 Mini	2	3	5
=124.	Chris Jones	2.o Mazda RX3 Coupé	2	3	5
=126.	Charles Bernstein	850 Mini	1	4	5
=126.	John Bury	1.3 MG Midget	1	4	5
=126.	Terry Harmer	1.3 Mini-Cooper S	1	4	5
=126.	Roger Matthews	1.0 Mini-Ford S	1	4	5
=126.	Paul Ratcliffe	848 Mini	1	4	5
=126.	John Targett	1.8 MGB	1	4	5
=132.	Brian Classick	5.3 Iso Grifo Bizzarini V8	—	5	5
=132.	Geoff Gilkes	850 Mini-Imp	—	5	5
=132.	Simon Kirkby	1.3 Simca Rallye 1	—	5	5
=132.	Geoff Lambert	1.6 FF Mallock U2- Holbay Mk 14	—	5	5
=132.	James Pinkerton	1.3 Mini-Cooper S	—	5	5
=132.	Clifford Watts	850 Hillman Imp	—	5	5
=132.	Barry Wood	1.1 Ginetta-Imp G15	—	5	5
139.	Tony Sugden	1.8 Ford Escort BDE	4	1 (—)	5 (4)
140.	Tim Wood	1.6 Magnum-Holbay C75	3	2 (1)	5 (4)
141.	Peter Pitman	1.0 Hillman Imp	2	3 (2)	5 (4)
=142.	Peter Richings	1.1 MG Midget	—	5 (4)	5 (4)
=142.	Andy McLennan	1.0 Austin A35	—	5 (4)	5 (4)
=142.	Colin Hesford	848 Mini/3.5 Morgan Plus 8	—	5 (4)	5 (4)

NB 1. All British and Irish races of less than National Open status plus all FF2000 events included.

NB 2. Figures in brackets represent total and class wins where there were at least three starters.

Racing Categories

Club racing can be described as motor racing for drivers whose interests are primarily the enjoyment of their sport, with monetary rewards or an easing of their costs being only of secondary consideration. Granted, most people today chase sponsorship and try to get someone else to pay for their racing to some degree, but one likes to feel that the true Club driver would use any money he may get to supplement his costs rather than to substitute for them.

Circuit racing has grown enormously since the circuit owners began promoting it in the mid '60s, and now there are literally hundreds of races and dozens of Championships for a driver to choose from. Yet the grids still stay full and even inflation, that dreaded disease of the '70s, has hardly halted the rush to the circuits.

There are three broad categories into which Club racing can be catalogued: Saloon car racing; Sports car racing; Single seater racing. The racing Saloons are all based on family(?) saloon cars and range from the little Renault 5's to the roaring Grand Prix engined devices seen in the Super Saloon Formula. But they all originated as road cars, no matter how tenuous at times the connection might seem.

The majority of the Sports cars are also derived from road machines, but not all of them. The cars built for the 750, 1300 and Clubmans formulae might ostensibly be two seaters, but no passenger could ever ride in them either in safety or comfort; indeed it is doubtful whether he could find a place in which to fit at all. So, far from road cars being turned into racing cars, these are racing cars half pretending to be road cars.

There is no doubt about the last category of Club racing however. The single seaters are just that; single seater cars built with just one object in view—to win races. This is where the aspiring professional will be found, and where the hardest races will be run.

In this book Formula 3 has not been included. In the '60s it could certainly have been numbered amongst Club formulae, but now costs have risen so astronomically that none but the very wealthy, the fully sponsored, or the man on his way up to a Formula 1 career, could ever hope to compete in more than just one or two races in a season. Yet there is another class of racing which has grown up to take its place; Formula Ford 1600. The ever popular Ford-engined single seaters have matured into a fully fledged racing formula where only the very best drivers can hope to succeed in such evenly matched cars.

In the following pages are listed the main formulae in the three categories of Club racing, and it is hoped that somewhere amongst the many different divisions and sub-divisions there will be a place for everyone who ever desired, or who ever wondered what it would be like, to go motor racing.

Mini Racing

Mini Racing in one form or another has been part of the Club racing scene now for incredibly, almost twenty years. Since Sir John Whitmore gave the Mini its competition debut at the Boxing Day Brands Hatch meeting in 1959, it has been a particular favourite with spectators and its versatility and cheapness have made it equally popular with the drivers.

Although the heyday of the Mini, Internationally at least, was in the mid '60s when it swept all before it in rallies and was no sluggard in racing either, the Mini still has a very firm place in Club racing and if anything its popularity is increasing. Certainly, since the return of the official Leyland interest in the little cars in 1976, Mini's are getting National exposure once again after a long period during which only the drivers and spectators were particularly interested in them.

In the early '60s a group of Morris Mini and Austin 7 enthusiasts formed the inevitable Mini 7 Club and having devised an 850cc racing formula, set up an annual National Championship based on the results of some 15 races held throughout the country. Just three years later, in answer to the eager cries of dozens of their Mini-Cooper brethren who wanted to play too, the Club organised the Mini Miglia (1000) Championship and this ran for many years in parallel with the Mini 7 Formula.

The two Classes became easily the most successful formula in terms of numbers of competitors in saloon car racing and the antics of the little Minis locked in combat around the circuits ensured that race organisers were always keen to add to their programmes any race in which Minis took part.

In mid-season of 1974 the Racing Centre of the Mini 7 Club joined with the London Centre of the Club to form the Mini 7 Racing Club which from then on continued the organisation and running of both racing formulae. This new Club still remains the 'racing' division of the parent Mini 7 Club.

In 1976 Leyland Cars joined with the Mini 7 Racing Club to initiate a more promotable series of Mini races and thus ostensibly return to motor racing without having to actually compete themselves. Sensibly they allowed the Club to administer and organise the "Leyland Cars Mini Challenge" which now, as well as the old 850 and 1000 Classes, includes a Class for 1275 GTs.

The regulations governing each formula are drawn up by the Mini 7 Racing Club and based on the views of competitors as well as race organisers and the sponsors. Leyland have restricted their technical involvement to a demand that to qualify for Championship points cars must be re-fitted with the radiator grills and other exterior appendages which had previously been removed to save weight and aid cooling.

The majority of the drivers have welcomed the return of B.M.C./B.L.M.C./British Leyland/Leyland Cars to racing as there are now some worthwhile prizes to be won. The overall National Champion (the competitor with the highest number of points in his Class), as well as picking up cash awards and Leyland Special Tuning spare parts vouchers on his way along the Championship trail, will pick up a new 1275 GT Mini for his efforts. There is also an annual Ladies award and there are cash prizes and trophies to be won by the winners of the three Championships; Mini 850, Mini 1000 and Mini 1275 GT.

In individual races too, trophies are awarded down to 4th place and Championship points down to 8th place. Each Class has an individual series of 18 races of which the best 14 score points for the Class and National Challenge, so there is no shortage of events for the more dedicated drivers.

It is a regulation requirement that drivers in any of the Classes must be members of the Mini 7 Racing Club before getting Championship points, but membership would also be of benefit to a driver not necessarily interested in the actual Championship.

Mini racing is not particularly cheap, at least not if you want to be in there doing the winning. Of course one can enter a virtually standard car and be content to finish out of the first ten, except when there are a massive number of retirements, but a stroll round the paddock and a careful look at the cars during a Mini race day will show the extraordinary amount of development which has gone into todays machines. Granted they *look* like standard cars from the spectator side of the fence, but close up . . . bonnets and front wings moulded in single fibreglass units which lift off in seconds; boots with the floor long gone in the interest of lightness and containing a small foam filled fuel tank on a tubular cradle; bootlids of fibreglass weighing only ounces and held in place by a rubber band; interiors gutted except for roll cage, fire extinguisher and the drivers seat; front and rear suspensions which are adjustable to give minute camber and castor changes; radiators mounted facing forward; massive oil breather catch tanks; and all this quite apart from engine modifications and dozens of other more personalised 'tweaks' all developed and built up during the Mini's long motor racing history.

The Mini racing people are a friendly lot and protests and scrutineering squabbles are rare. Most of them do their own preparation and maintenance and usually keep the same car and stay in the same Class, season after season. Their immediate goal is usually the shaving of odd fractions off their lap times by constant playing about with engine mods. and suspension settings so as to pursue and pass the chap who beat them the previous weekend.

This is an excellent formula in which to learn 'racemanship' and the importance of car preparation; even a difference of one degree in rear wheel pre-race adjustment can show up as a difference of several seconds at the end of a ten lap race. The cars are not all that slow either; even the 850's have a top speed of over a hundred miles an hour and the 1000's and 1275's are very much quicker.

It is not yet known for how long Leyland Cars will sponsor the Mini Challenge, but with nearly 20 years of racing behind them it looks as though the future of Mini racing is assured and they will remain, for competitors, the most popular form of saloon car racing for a long time yet to come.

Production Saloons

Saloon car racing of any description has always been

enormously popular with British race-going enthusiasts. Whether the cars were the huge American Galaxies of over a decade ago which mixed it with everything from Jaguars to Austin Cambridges, Morris Minors and Austin A35's; or the Superspeed entered 105E Anglias which diced so brilliantly with the B.M.C. Mini's in the mid '60s; or the highly individual antics of the great Jim Clark in Colin Chapmans Lotus Cortinas towards the end of the '60s; the start of the saloon car race at any meeting could always be guaranteed to bring spectators, mechanics, drivers from other races and any of the officials and marshalls not actually working, rushing to the fence in eager anticipation of the invariably exciting opening laps.

It has been said many times that the main reason that Production Saloon racing in particular is so popular is that the spectators can identify more easily with the familiar looking cars than with those in any other form of racing. Certainly the cars, at least on the surface, look the same as the ones the spectators arrive at the circuits in, and many an inter-make battle has been extended to the road home, long after the races are over.

Manufacturers have long supported Saloon Car racing, either officially or through their dealers or through well established semi-private race preparation specialists, and so most of the drivers in present day Production Saloons tend to be contracted for the whole season. Sadly, this 'professionalism' has led to an inordinate amount of rule bending and blatant cheating which has made the inevitable post race protests and scrutineering more important in deciding race winners than the races themselves. Luckily only the more knowledgable spectators are aware of the misdeeds of the over-eager few, and hopefully commercialism might make way just a little in time for the apparently forgotten axiom that how you win is every bit as important as whether you win.

Ostensibly modern Production Saloon Car racing is for standard production saloons or what the F.I.A. (motorsports international controlling body, the Federation International de l'Automobile) calls Group 1. The word 'ostensibly' is used because several problems arise when one tries to race standard cars.

On the surface it would seem that cars "straight from the show-room" would provide ideal inter-make comparison racing, would be relatively cheap, could even, perhaps, be driven to and from the circuit and, most important of all, would be completely free of protest as any apparent ambiguity could be speedily resolved by checking against a similar 'showroom' model.

Racing however, puts stresses on cars which would seldom, if ever, be experienced on the road. Hub-caps for example (although thankfully these are at last disappearing from road cars), would fly like Frisbees into the crowd if they were left on cars which periodically 'lean' on each other while racing; standard brake linings and brake fluid would hardly last five laps before fading and boiling; tool-kits would fly about in the boot and would probably be joined by the spare wheel; and the standard lap and diagonal seat belts would never keep the poor driver securely in place during a high speed roll.

Basically a manufacturer must have produced 5000 examples of a particular car for it to be eligible for Group 1, and any optional extras fitted for racing such as disc brakes or servos must also have been produced in similar quantity. Production proof is declared by the manufacturer to the F.I.A. who issue 'Forms of Recognition' or, as they are more usually known, Homolugation papers. These are necessary before the car can legally compete.

Sometimes the F.I.A. sends a representative to the factory to check that the manufacturers' claims are not just figments of his imagination, but there have been occasions when these inspections must have been very cursory indeed.

In Great Britain the R.A.C. modifies the International rules to suit national circumstances and to try to make the racing more interesting and meaningful to the British car buying public. During the early '70s the cars were divided by retail price groups into four main Classes, but inflation caused the prices to change year by year and then almost month by month so that different cars became, at least on paper, eligible for different classes almost too often for the powers that be to keep up. This meant that while the racing was always exciting it became increasingly difficult to keep any degree of consistency in the class structure between cars in the same price range. However, the idea was basically a good one and it was a pity that for 1977 it was mooted that the class divisions be changed back to cubic capacity groups.

A further rather clever requirement was made by the R.A.C. for entries in Production Saloons. Cars had to be generally available for retail purchase in the United Kingdom and had to be listed in the annual Buyers Guide published by the magazine *Autocar.* Cars which were dropped from production and consequently from the Buyers Guide, would be allowed to race for a further year but from then on would be ineligible. Also cars had to run to the specification as marketed in the U.K. and no optional equipment was permitted.

Modifications permitted in Production Saloon racing include:

The fitting of specialised drivers seats (many standard seats collapsed even in relatively mild accidents).

Fitting oil baffles in the sump (oil surge ruined several engines).

Removing exhausts (this was done not alone to increase efficiency, but to give the spectators more noise for their money).

Fitting stronger shock absorbers (standard ones allow the cars to roll like a blancmange and anyway wear out too quickly).

Fitting of an oil-cooler (even carefully built and 'blue-printed' standard engines without oil coolers do not take kindly to racing).

A full roll-over cage must be fitted inside the cars.

Fire extinguishers carrying at least 5 kilograms must be fitted.

An externally mounted battery cut-off switch must be fitted in a prominent position (so that safety marshalls can turn off the electrics from outside the car if the driver can't do it from the inside).

Racing tyres are prohibited but there is a vast selection of road tyres, approved by the R.A.C., from which drivers can chose whichever type they feel might give them an advantage.

Engine modifications in Production Saloon racing are strictly prohibited and engines must comply to manufacturers specifications. Now while this might sound simple enough, in effect it means that as 'manufacturers specifications' allow certain machining and fitting tolerances both in original manufacture and in replacement parts, a clever engine specialist can gain an appreciable power increase in rebuilding a standard engine by taking maximum advantage of these tolerances. This specialised engine building is now colloquially known as 'blue-printing', because the manufacturers original drawings or blue-prints are used extensively for reference.

All this unfortunately means that professional race preparation specialists are much in demand in order to extract every possible power advantage from the engines of the leading cars. This, of course, involves much expense and rather defeats the object of the Group 1 exercise.

Because engine tuning is limited to 'blue-printing' and careful balancing resulting in, theoretically at least, matched performances from similar cars, even the smallest difference in b.h.p. output can make a difference to race results. This has led to some very liberal interpretation of the rules and the R.A.C. scrutineers have had to take an increasingly stronger stand against continuing rule bending and cheating.

There is now an R.A.C. rule that cars may be chosen at

random during the season to undergo stringent eligibility inspection. Any infringment of the rules in the eyes of the scrutineers will mean that all championship points gained up to that time will be forfeited. The inspections are made at the tracks but in cases where the actual engine or suspension parts have to be stripped down, the scrutineers have the power to seal the component parts in situ until they are ready to begin their inspection. Should a driver subsequently be unfortunate enough to present a damaged or missing seal he will not alone lose all points gained in the championship up to that time, he will be excluded from the championship for the remainder of the season.

A lot of extra enthusiasm for Production Saloon racing was created by B.B.C. Radio One who sponsored one of the two year-long Championships for the Formula in 1975 and '76. The Championship was further promoted by Noel Edmonds, one of B.B.C's disc jockeys who competed enthusiastically in most of the races and who invariably mentioned the racing on his Monday morning radio shows. The B.B.C's efforts attracted a much wider audience than had hitherto watched saloon car racing and by introducing pop stars and disc jockeys to the circuits with various side shows and a general circus type atmosphere, pushed the circuit attendances far higher on several occasions than the pure promotion of the races themselves would ever have managed.

Outside Production Saloon racing, Group 1 is virtually non-existent so unless a driver commits himself to one of the Championships his saloon racing will have to be limited to either Classic of Special Saloons, or one of the one-make series of races which appear from time to time such as Renault 5 or Ford Escort. The only other alternative would be to drive in one of the Mini Classes.

If, on the other hand, a driver decides that Group 1 is the place to be, it must be with the realisation that it's going to cost a lot of money in race preparation to get amongst the leaders, and a lot of money will probably have to be spent

1 Mini 1000 racing at Cadwell Park

2 The cheapest class in Production Saloon racing has always provided the greatest variety in cars entered. Over the past few years, Moskvich, Sunbeam Imp, Simca Rallye, Lada 1200, Mini Clubman G.T. and, as here, Honda Civic have all, at one time or another shown up well in this well supported class

3 *above*   North London Policeman Trevor Moore drives this Avenger well above the speed limit in Production Saloon Racing

4 *below*   Production Saloon Car racing at Brands Hatch. Noel Edmunds (Opel Commodore), Ivan Dutton (Ford Capri), and Bob Saunders (Triumph Dolomite)

5 *above* Arthur Collier's Skoda and Gerry Marshall's Vauxhall in a round of the highly entertaining Special Saloon formula at Thruxton

6 *below* A super example of a Special Saloon formula car. Colin Hawker's Volkswagen with Formula 1 Cosworth/Ford engine

7 *below* It's really a Ford Escort—albeit a Special Saloon one—at a wet Oulton Park

8 Super Saloons provide a unique outlet for ingenuity, engineering, eccentricity and, naturally, money. Tony Hazle-woods incredible Jaguar with its ex-Surtees full race Chevrolet engine mounted amidships, is a superb example

9 The engine in the Hazlewood Jaguar/Chevrolet makes very few concessions to the driver

10 Super Saloon formula, 2-litre Cosworth/Ford engined Hillman Imp of Jonathan Buncombe

ironing out the many dings in the bodywork which will result from the inevitable crashes which occur in this very commercialised branch of Club racing.

Special Saloons

Special Saloon car racing is a National formula for Groups 1 and 2 saloon cars and for any other cars which might not actually have been homologated with the F.I.A. but which the R.A.C. has verified have been produced in sufficient quantities to qualify. In Group 1 the minimum number manufactured to qualify (as in Production Saloons) is 5000 and in Group 2, just 1000. Both Groups are for saloon cars with four seats and engines of over 700cc capacity. If under 700cc (so remote a chance as to be almost non-existent) the car need only have two seats.

The F.I.A. engine and bodywork restrictions on both Groups are waived for this National formula, and unlimited mechanical modifications are allowed. Even a completely different engine from a different car can be fitted, the only stipulation here being that the engine and gearbox must be kept at the same end of the car as originally intended by the manufacturer.

Bodywork restrictions are limited to the retaining of the standard profile, or silhouette, of the car when viewed from the side, above a hypothetical line drawn between the front and rear wheel centres. This doesn't apply to either the bonnet or boot lid, which can be any shape the builder/designer wishes. Air spoilers can be fitted to the boot lid, but not wings. The difference between spoilers and wings, according to the 'Blue Book', being that spoilers should have no forward facing gaps between the spoiler and the boot lid and should merely be a raised surface on the boot lid.

Special Saloons are divided into four seperate Classes according to engine capacity: up to 850cc; from 850cc to 1000cc; from 1000cc to 1300cc; and over 1300cc. There is a strong possibility that in the future there will be an upper capacity limit of between 2 and 3 litres; cars above this limit will then be eligible for what the R.A.C. has suggested be called a 'Free Formula'. This has all stemmed from the, almost breakaway, Super Saloon faction which is, at least as far as the R.A.C. is concerned, in a sort of established formulae limbo. However, all this may not happen and Special Saloons and Super Saloons may well be able to develop in parallel and become equally popular in their own right.

Many ingeniously designed and beautifully built cars have appeared in the Championships run annually for Special Saloons. In the 1300cc Class, Ford Twin-Cam engines, reduced from their standard engine cubic capacity, have been fitted not only in Escorts which is logical enough, but in several highly competitive Mini's. Space-frame Imps and Anglias have been built for the 1000cc Class (the Anglia with a small belt-drive Twin-Cam Escort engine), and a Fiat 850 Coupé body was popped on to a Merlyn ex-Formula 3 chassis powered by a 1 litre Holbay racing engine and driven to several wins by Derek Walker.

Imps and Minis have dominated the 850cc Class but even here convention has been ignored by Geoff Gilkes who has successfully combined the best of both worlds by powering his Mini with an Imp engine.

The biggest Class in Special Saloons (over 1300cc tends to be a hunting ground for Ford Capris and the bigger Vauxhalls which, because of their inherent power and performance, tend not to attract the ingenious attention and modification that characterises their lower capacity brethren.

Special Saloon drivers are not plagued by the constant struggle to increase performance without affecting Group 1 Specifications, which so affects their Production Saloon racing colleagues. Consequently there are fewer scrutineering problems and eligibility protests are thankfully rare. The racing is always fast and usually furious and with some half a dozen different annual Championships giving a massive total of around 70 races, it is the most prolific branch of saloon car racing.

Super Saloons

A highly popular branch of Special Saloon racing, Super Saloon racing began in 1974. At that time quite a few of the Special Saloons were being built to rather more 'way out' specifications than were strictly necessary, or indeed legal, and one of the builder/drivers, Tony Hazlewood, decided to run a race for these 'Super' Saloons.

Hazlewood, who comes from High Wycombe and who still competes himself in a Formula 5000 bellowing monster he calls a Jaguar XJ-8, organised the first race at Silverstone and managed to collect a grid of over 20 cars which competed for a purse made up of the £50's which each of the competitors contributed to the prize kitty.

The cars come mainly from the growing number of V-8 engined saloons which had been built to compete in the several Special Saloon Championships being run at the time. The drivers were eager to run in a Championship of their own but in spite of the success of the first race and the few other races which were run in 1974, it wasn't until the following year that the big cars were properly organised.

For 1975 a proper season-long Championship for Super Saloons was set up and run by the B.R.S.C.C. with sponsorship coming from Tricentrol Ltd., of London. Some amazing cars appeared, and the ingenuity and engineering required to get some of them on the road, let alone racing, could only be wondered at.

Gerry Marshall won the first full years Championship with a 5 litre Repco-Holden racing engine nestling in his ex-1974 Vauxhall Firenza. The car, built by Bill Blydenstein of Dealer Team Vauxhall, and affectionately known as "Baby Bertha" went like a tornado and just about blew everything else off the road.

Other cars appearing in the first year as Super Saloons included John Turners 5 litre rear-engined Skoda; Alec Poole's Skoda powered by a racing 2 litre Ford engine; Nick Whiting's space-frame Escort; Colin Hawkers Cosworth Formula 1 engined Volkswagen beetle with Brabham Formula 1 suspension; a 7.2 litre Chevrolet engined Ford Capri; an 8.1 Chevrolet Corvair and Tony Hazlewood's Daf-Oldsmobile.

In 1975 the R.A.C. ran a round of the Championship as a supporting race for the British Grand Prix at Silverstone which, instead of giving the Super Saloons (or 'Superloons' as one apparently American inspired genius suggested they be called) a deserved boost and an added respectability, proved to be a bit of a disaster. Many of the cars were still in the early stages of development and quite a few failed to turn up for the race. Of those that did actually start, only a handful lasted the full race distance and the eventual winner, Gerry Marshall in 'Big Bertha' finished so far in front that, in spite of the few interesting battles which took place further down the field, the whole thing looked to be a bit of a farce.

The R.A.C. were, understandably perhaps, a little put out by the disappointing performance of cars which had, on paper at least, shown such crowd pleasing promise, and since then have not looked too kindly on Super Saloons. However, the Championship backers Tricentrol, were happy enough and continued to offer sponsorship into 1976. Certainly the competitors themselves are still building bigger and faster cars to previously undreamed of specifications and continue to provide some of the best Club racing to be seen on the circuits. Indeed a visit to a race meeting where the bellowing monsters are appearing should be completed not just by enjoying the sound and fury of the amazing cars, but by a visit to the Paddock to view at close hand the beautiful workmanship and design which has gone into their construction.

Super Saloons are run to the same basic rules as Special

Saloons but there is a 1600cc minimum engine capacity limit. The cars tend to be really extrovert machines with equally extrovert drivers who race the big noisy machines for the sheer hell of it, but because of this, as the cars get more and more complex, they naturally get more expensive and it is difficult to see where the future lies. The cost of building the cars is enormous, even for those lucky enough to have their own garages or workshops, and once built, the cars still need a constant input of time, effort and money to keep them competitive and reliable. Surprisingly, too, some of the circuit owners have been rather indifferent to Super Saloons, perhaps because of the British G.P. experience, but with the increasing reliability of the cars and the appearance of new and more outlandish models they are coming round to the realisation that Super Saloons, if properly promoted, could be a very big crowd puller indeed.

Tricentrol however, (the word was used originally as the Telex sign-off of Trinidad Central Oilfields, which was the parent company of the present huge International conglomerate) have done a lot to help the drivers costs. It may be expensive to run in Super Saloons but the prize money is about the most generous in Club racing and at around £500 per race, gives the entries something realistic to aim for.

The B.R.S.C.C. is the organising club for the annual Championship series of races but it may be that the newly formed Super Saloon Drivers Association, if given sufficient support and encouragement, might eventually be able to take over this role for themselves.

It would be a great shame if the big cars were to fade from the Club scene. The Americans have for long enjoyed the sight and sound of their big 'stockers' at tracks like Talledega and Daytona, and if Super Saloon racing in this country can survive its difficult formative years and become more firmly established in Club racing, then it must surely attract the massive enthusiast following that it so richly deserves.

Classic Saloon Cars

Classic Saloon racing has got to be the great fun formula of the '70s. Conceived by Peter Deffee, who had a Mk.7 Jaguar all dressed up with nowhere to go, the cars had their first full Championship in 1975 and were immediately successful with spectators and competitors alike.

Classic Saloon Cars as defined by the regulations are production saloon cars which were marketed before March 1957. The include Jaguars; Ford Zephyrs; Wolseleys; Lancias; Borgwards; Rileys; Mercedes; Jowetts; M.G. Magnettes; and a seemingly endless succession of Morris Minors and Austin A35's.

The cars are kept as standard as possible and provide cheap and entertaining racing for as cheerful and extrovert a bunch of enthusiasts as are to be found anywhere in Club racing. Advertising on the cars is frowned upon, and it is recommended that cars 'be presented with a high standard of appearance, both inside and out, preferably to manufacturers specifications'.

The Classic Car Club, formed to look after the needs of the happy racers, has drawn up a short list of rules and regulations which are designed to keep the cars as near standard as possible, and to discourage any suggestion of professionalism. The following are extracts:

All competitors must be members of the Classic Saloon Car Club who issue a full list of eligible cars.

Classes are:

(a) Over 2700cc
(b) 1902cc to 2700cc
(c) 1252cc to 1901cc
(d) Up to 1251cc

All vehicles must comply with R.A.C Vehicle Regulations and must comply with current M.O.T. Regulations and hold an M.O.T. Test Certificate.

Bodywork must be entirely standard and complete, and all radiator grills, bumpers and over-riders, and brightwork to original specification must be retained.

Chassis, suspension and engine must be retained in standard form except for a few minor exceptions.

Choice of clutch, gearbox and steering is free.

Road wheel rim width is free but these are usually kept fairly standard as no alterations are permitted to the mudguards. Only road tyres are permitted.

Carpets and the rear seat squab can be removed but the dashboard, front seats, interior trim, and window and door mechanisms must be retained.

It can be seen from these few regulations that the main aim of the Club is to keep the racing as uncomplicated as possible, consistent with discouraging the odd gentleman who might feel like ignoring the spirit of the regulations so as to win races. Happily, such gentlemen are as yet unknown in Classic Saloons, and this bodes well for the future.

This formula must be thoroughly recommended for anyone who cannot afford any of the more exotic branches of Club racing and who has just sufficient rudimentary knowledge of ordinary car mechanics to build himself a car from, say, the darkest depths of his local second-hand car showroom. Or, perhaps better still, buy two or three models from a scrap-yard, use the best parts from each one and build up a car that way. The car could always be used as a second road car.

Escorts and Renault 5 Challenges

Escorts

Organised by the all-encompassing B.R.S.C.C., the Ford Escort Challenge is run for Mk 1 Escort Mexico's and, since 1975, Mk 2 Escort Sport 1600's. Cars are run to F.I.A. Group 1 specification, but the Sport model is allowed stiffer front springs and minor carburettor modifications so as to make its performance similar to the slightly faster Mexico. Only very limited engine modifications are allowed (or attempted-honestly!) and the tyres must be Dunlop Intermediates, i.e. for wet or dry use.

The formula has been running since the early'70s, and is now pretty well established in its own right as one of the least expensive forms of saloon car racing. Granted, there is something slightly 'gimmicky' about one-make cars running to a very limited specification, but many of the competitors claim that if it were not for the Escort Challenge, they could not afford to go motor racing at all. Certainly the Escort has always been an extremely easy car to work on, and repairs and servicing can be carried out much more easily and at less expense than on almost any other car, whether it be used either on the track or on the road.

The cars are very forgiving to drive too, and although there will always be one or two drivers who shine above the rest in any class of motor racing, there is always good close racing to be seen right through the field in Escort events.

Because the cars are all from the same manufacturer, there is none of the inter-make political bickering that goes on in other formulae, and thus the emphasis is on driver against driver contests rather than car against car.

This is very much an amateur formula and while most drivers manage to get a certain amount of sponsorship these days from somewhere or other, in the Escort Challenge this tends to be low key and only on rare occasions raises its head.

The B.R.S.C.C. runs an annual Championship of some 16 races, ranging from Croft and Rufforth in the North, to Llandow in the West and Brands Hatch in the South East. Cash rewards are not great, less than £40 for a 1st place in any of the races and £250 for the over all Championship winner, but the racing, as we have said before, is good, protests are few and the cars are amongst the easiest of all to keep in tip-top condition.

The formula looks like having a secure future (although with the original Mexico now out of production probably more use will have to be made of later models) and with this in mind, together with the benefits we have already mentioned, Escort racing in this category must be considered to be one of the most ideal formulae for a newcomer to motor racing.

Renault 5

The Renault 5 Challenge is an interesting formula if only because it is so quiet! It is organised by the B.R.S.C.C. who run it within the framework of the F.I.A. Group 1 regulations, and even open exhausts are banned, hence the quietness. But this does not in any way detract from the racing which, because of the B.R.S.C.C.'s strict control and the consequent similarity in the performance of the cars, is extremely close and exciting.

The formula is open to Renault 5TL saloons, except those with sunshine roofs, equipped to catalogue specifications as marketed in the U.K. Michelin tyres are mandatory as is a safety kit including laminated screen, roll-over bar etc., marketed by Renault themselves.

The incredible angles at which the little cars bustle round corners make them very good value for spectators, and with grids of up to 30 cars starting some of the races, the activity at the first couple of corners is always worth watching.

This is a rather specialised formula and while the cars can be fun to drive, they can be expensive to repair and maintain. It is doubtful therefore that it would be of interest to drivers not specifically interested in Renaults or their promotion. For those who *are* interested though, the B.R.S.C.C. run a season-long Championship along Escort Challenge lines with similar prizes and an equal number of races.

750 Formula

Originally formed to cater for the 'impecunious enthusiast' with particular reference to the Austin Seven owner, the

750 Motor Club has grown from strength to strength over the years, without ever losing sight of its original objectives: simplicity and low cost.

Of course the Austin Seven in question was not the modern Mini, as we know it, but that delightful little car from between the wars which so endeared itself to a whole generation of first time motorists.

The Austin Seven was rather like a grown-up Meccanno set. Thousands of young men had one as their first car, and hundreds modify them for more speed or stripped and completely rebuilt them. They were used as the basis for not only race cars, but also Trials Specials, Sprint and Rally cars. Colin Chapman, founder of Lotus, first started his competition career in an Austin 7 Special. It was a 1930 Austin 7 Fabric Saloon, which his turned into a Trials special, retaining the engine, gearbox, axles and brakes. It first competed in 1948. Now the creator of that Austin 7 special has numerous world championships to his credit. In a smaller, or rather in not such a big way, many other well-known personalities have started their competition careers in home-built 750 specials. And what an excellent training ground.

The formula began when, after the last war, it was found that the cost of sports car racing began to escalate rapidly out of the hands of all but the privileged few. Austin Seven racing enthusiasts at the time were naturally lucky in that their costs and expenses were probably cheapest of all, but they found it difficult to find a class of racing to suit their particular needs. In 1949 Holland Birkett, Chairman of the 750 Motor Club devised a limiting formula for Austin Seven cars and having persuaded race organisers that events would be supported in sufficient numbers to make them worthwhile, ran the first race for the new formula at Silverstone in 1950.

The formula proved a huge success, and for many years races were run for Austin Seven specials at meetings throughout the country, but inevitably as time went by

Austin Seven cars and parts became dearer and more difficult to find.

Originally the formula laid down that the cars must retain at least the side members of the Austin Seven chassis and that the back axle be from an Austin Seven. This was changed so that home-made chassis might be used together with a different axle, although both were still limited in type and design. A substitute for the engine was a little more difficult but it was found that the engines in the Reliant range of 3-wheeler cars were an ideal substitute, and so the formula continued to live, albeit under the slightly different title of the Reliant 750 Formula, although still run by the 750 Motor Club.

The Club also runs two other formulae which although not as cheap as 750 racing still provide a relatively inexpensive introduction to motor racing; Formula 1300 and Formula 4. Their three formulae are all aimed at the man with limited money, but who has ingenuity, patience and a capacity for hard work. This is a club which actively promotes home design and home construction of racing cars. This can mean very cheap racing, and can give great satisfaction to the designer/constructor/driver. Commercialism is banned, advertising strictly limited and professional maintenance prohibited.

Reliant 750 Formula

Chassis: Home built and designed two-seater sports car, front or rear engined, with two longitudinal chassis members of 2-inch square steel on to which the suspension is mounted. These are similar to the old Austin 7 side members.

Engine: The engine most used is the Reliant 748cc OHV, though the 600cc OHV and 747cc SV and Austin 747cc SV are also eligible. However, since the beginning of 1965 no *new* cars will be eligible if fitted with side valve engines. On the Reliant OHV engine, the cylinder block and crank

case and cylinder head castings must be standard items, but may be modified. The stroke and bore must remain unchanged. No additions to combustion chambers is permitted, and ports must remain in the original place. Choice of camshaft is free. A restrictor of 22mm internal diameter must be fitted between the carburettor and the manifold. On the smaller 642cc engine the restrictor diameter is 28mm (only to the end of 1976).
Gearbox: 4 gears and reverse.
Axle: A proprietary live axle (Morris Minor/Austin A35 are popular). Lightweight components and limited slip differentials not allowed.

Body and safety requirements are set out in the R.A.C. Year Book and we need not go into detail here. Perhaps the best guide to the formula is the statement by the Club itself: "The formula was devised for the benefit of the amateur driver, constructor and tuner with limited resources. The 750 Motor Club therefore reserves the right at all times to reject any car which it considers represents an attempt to defeat the spirit of the regulations even though it complies with the letter of them".

750 racing has managed to continue as it started, with its main aims and aspirations still intact. It is tremendously popular and during 1975 alone no less than eighty-six different competitors scored points in the Championship run by the Club.

Although not amongst the fastest of cars the quicker examples still manage to lap the Brands Hatch Club circuit at close to 80mph, and the events invariably provide close competitive racing.

For further information regarding the cars and championships write to Iain Millar, 9 Westmeare, The Thorpe, Hemingford Grey, Huntingdon PE18 9BZ.

Formula 1300

Formula 1300, like its younger brother Formula 750, has its

origins in the search for an inexpensive form of Motor racing after the last war. Towards the end of the 40s and the beginning of the 50s, the 750 Motor Club decided to devise a new class of racing which would be a step up from the Austin 7 based and already established, 750 Formula. Beginning in 1952 as Formula 1200, the new cars were limited to using the 1172cc Ford E93A or 100E side valve engine, but chassis design choice was completely free. The new Formula, just as Formula 750, stimulated designers and constructors into producing all manner of weird and wonderful machines and it became a breeding ground for now internationally known names, such as Len Terry, Eric Broadly and Colin Chapman. As the years went by and side valve engines in general, and the 1172cc engine in particular, became more difficult to find, so a change was made to allow the use of the more easily obtainable overhead valve engines.

The cars are basically two-seater sports cars with either front or rear engine, and with open or closed body work. There are no chassis restrictions other than that no proprietary rear-engined cars built after 1st January 1971 are allowed. Engine choice is restricted to either the Ford 1200cc, overhead valve engine from the deluxe 105E Anglia, or the bigger 1300cc, overhead valve engine which, if used, must be fitted with a carburettor restrictor to reduce its power output to that of the 1200 unit. On both engines the standard block and cylinder head must be retained, but they can be modified and this, together with a free choice of camshaft, gives interesting scope for home engine tuners. Racing tyres are not permitted and neither are wings.

There is plenty of scope for original thinking in the Formula and most of the winning cars are home built specials. The 1975 Formula 1300 Champion car was basically designed and built by its owner/driver who also built the engine. At the end of the year it was reckoned that the season of twenty races had cost him in the region of

£1,000, not of course counting the cost of the car, which goes to show that the Formula really must be one of the cheapest ways for club drivers to go motor racing in a pure racing car.

Second-hand cars rarely make their way into the magazine classifieds, and those that do are generally snapped up pretty quickly. However one that appeared during the middle of the 1976 season with over thirty wins to its credit, complete and ready to go, was on offer for £850.

There is an annual championship, run by the 750 club, which is based on some twenty events and further details regarding the championship can be had from The 750 Motor Club, Director for F1300 Affairs, Bryan Clayton, 39 Cannon Grove, Fetcham, Leatherhead, Surrey KT22 9LG.

Generally this is a well supported formula, which although perhaps not as popular as the 750 Formula, reflects the increasing demand for a low cost form of motor racing. Although this is yet another example of the 750 Motor Club's low cost approach to motor racing, these little sports cars are by no means amongst the slowest on the track. Their lap record on the Brands Hatch short circuit now stands at over 85mph, and the car which we have already mentioned, which won the 1975 1300 Championship has lapped Castle Coombe at over 95mph.

Clubmans Formula

Devised in 1965 by the B.A.R.C. and the B.R.S.C.C., the Clubmans Formula began with rules specifically framed to take in the Lotus 7, Mallock U2, D.R.W. and other small engined Sports Cars of the time. The cars were nearly all using 1 litre B.M.C. or Ford engines, and the main object of the Formula was to allow the little cars to compete in races against their own kind, rather than against the more sophisticated rear engined sports racers of the '60s.

Two of the great cornerstones of the Clubmans Formula

were Colin Chapman and Arthur Mallock. Chapman, one of the 750 Motor Club's more successful graduates, had designed cars for the Clubs Austin 7 and Ford 1172 formulae and from these had grown the Lotus 7. Mallock, the ex-army 'Mad Major' had also designed and built cars, not only for the 750 Formula but also for Formula Junior, the Ford Championship of Ireland and Formula 2. Both Chapmans Lotus 7 and Mallocks U2 (he called most of his cars "U 2's" at the time and the name derived from his idea that 'you too can go motor racing cheaply') were the mainstay of the new Formula during its formative years.

Engine specification remained largely unchanged until 1974 when the 1600cc Formula Ford engine was allowed to be used. This was a substitute for the almost universally used 1 litre ex Formula 3 racing units which were by then becoming very difficult to find and maintain.

At present there are two Classes in Clubmans racing, the limiting factor in both Classes being the 1600cc capacity limit on the engine.

Class A allows fully modified 1600cc engines to any specification provided that the cylinder head and block are from the engine manufacturers original production components. Engines can be of B.L.M.C.; Ford G.B.; Chrysler U.K. or General Motors U.K. origin, but the most common engine used is Ford. Fuel injection is prohibited but none the less the majority of the faster engines manage to deliver over 160 b.h.p.

Class B engines comply with current Formula Ford specifications. Body design still follows the basic design requirements of over ten years ago in that they are front engined, open body-work, two seater, sports racing cars. Either tubular or monocoque chassis are allowed but generally builders stick to the simpler and cheaper tubular format. Gearboxes may have no more than four forward speeds derived from the same manufacturers previously mentioned and gearboxes with rapidly interchangable ratios, like the Hewland racing box, are not allowed.

Suspension design is free and variations which have appeared include conventional unequal length wishbones; transverse rear springs; rising rate linkages with inboard front disc brakes and de Dion back axles. Limited slip or locked differentials are not allowed.

There is a mandatory cockpit width of 32-in (ostensibly wide enough for two people) but in effect the passenger space is usually taken up with spare fuel tanks or fire extinguishers. Rear wings are allowed but are limited in size, and safety requirements range from roll-over bars to safety belts and, of all things, a red tail-light to be used in the event of 'inclement weather'.

Clubmans racing offers a lot of scope for the budding racing car designer. The suspension can be as sophisticated as that of any single seater and there is more to be gained from experimenting with the wing angles and size as well as the general aerodynamics than in almost any other formula. Although it is mandatory that the cars be front engined, they do not have to be built to a low weight limit and so the designer/driver can play around with weight reduction and distribution in an effort to increase performance.

The Formula was planned specifically for the British Club driver and is not in any way International, although there have been some thoughts of introducing it overseas where it is hoped by the Clubmans Register that it might replace Continental 2 litre Sports Car racing. The majority of the competitors are not really using Clubmans as a stepping stone to greater things and are generally content to keep as their goal the gaining of points in whichever Championship they may be running in. This is not to say that the formula might not be a good one for the aspiring professional instead of the more obvious Formula Ford, as at least the Clubmans cars are quite a bit faster.

There are at least three different Championships run for the cars during the season and a driver should be able to get in twenty to twenty five races between March and October.

To its great credit the Clubmans Formula has continued to be the most sophisticated and quickest of the many cheaper classes of Club racing. The cars are very quick indeed and the Class A cars can now be reckoned to be able to lap the Silverstone Grand Prix circuit at around 115 m.p.h.

Clubmans racing is by no means one of the cheapest forms of Club racing, and the leading cars can cost far more to build or buy and then maintain than a Formula Ford. The drivers are generally a cheerful bunch who tend to look upon themselves as being a little mad or possibly eccentric. In the main they are dedicated amateurs; but dedicated more to enjoying themselves in cars which they mould to match their own whims rather than in cars built to an inflexible formula such as Formula Ford or even Formula 3.

Production Sports Cars

Conceived by the B.R.S.C.C. and M.C.D. as a sports car equivalent of the highly successful Production Saloon racing formula, the Production Sports Cars formula was launched in 1973. It got off to a poor start as no overall sponsor was found for the Championship and the races were dominated by Porsches in the first year and an expensive Pantera in 1974. Banning the big, expensive cars and putting an upper price limit on the cars eligible for the Championship, changed the whole scene for 1975 and since then it has been very successful.

Production Sports Cars (or Prod Sports as they are more commonly known) race in a formula registered by the B.R.S.C.C. for the use of its members. The Club produces a list of eligible cars each year and decides the price limits for the Classes. There are two Championships, one in the North at Croft, Rufforth and Cadwell Park and the other at six different Southern circuits.

Naturally prices change year by year, but the following eligibility list for 1976 will give an idea of what cars one might expect to find in the three Classes into which they are divided:

Class A £3,000 to £4,500.
Datsun: 240Z; 260Z; 260Z 2+2.
Jaguar: E type 4.2; E type V-12.
Jensen Healey.
Lotus: Elan+2; Elan+2S; Elan S4; Elan Sprint; Europa Twin-Cam; Europa Special.
MGB: V8 G.T.
Morgan: +8.
Triumph: Stag.
TVR: 3000M.

Class B £2,000 to £3,000.
Ginetta: G15.
MGB: 1800.
Morgan: 4/4 (1600cc).
Triumph: G.T.6, Mk2 & M3.
TVR: 1600.

Class C up to £2,000.
Austin Healey: Sprite Mk4 (1275cc).
MG: Midget 1500, Midget Mk3 & Mk4 (1275cc).
Triumph: Spitfire 1500; Spitfire Mk3 & Mk4 (1296cc).

The list of cars is taken (like Production Saloons) from the *Autocar* Buyers Guide of the current or of previous years, and the price includes V.A.T. and Car Tax. Cars must be equipped (with certain exceptions stipulated by the B.R.S.C.C.) as they are, or were, on offer to retail buyers. The immediate past predecessors of current models may be eligible but they must be equipped as per their original specification.

Cars must comply with F.I.A. Group 1 regulations, apart

from the B.R.S.C.C. regulations, and must not be fitted with any extra cost optional performance equipment, whether it be Homologated or not, apart from lightweight body panels, overdrive and anti-roll bars.

The B.R.S.C.C. say of the formula: 'The cars must adhere to the manufacturers specification of their lowest priced model, and any modifications are limited by the regulations. Shock absorbers may be changed and the engine can be blue-printed, but other than that, and necessary safety precautions, the cars performing in Production Sports Car racing are pretty close to their equivalents in the local car showrooms, right down to the use of road tyres'.

The basic regulations are

1 Exhaust system beyond the standard exhaust manifold is free.

2 The spare wheel and the tool kit need not be carried.

3 The generator (alternator) must not be changed and must work.

4 A safety fuel tank may be fitted.

5 The fuel filler may be modified.

6 The weight of the car must be within 5 per cent of that given in the *Autocar* Buyers Guide.

7 The steering wheel may be changed.

8 The ground clearance must not be less than 1-in below standard.

9 The drivers seat may be changed.

10 The carpets and felt may be removed.

11 The narrowest wheel rim width specified by the manufacturers must be used.

12 The tyres must be as listed in the manufacturers specification.

13 Engine oil baffles may be fitted.

What is really interesting about this Class of racing is that it is designed for near standard *road* sports cars, and a good proportion of the competitors drive their cars to the circuits. Here then is a perfect formula for the financially not so well-off would-be competitor; he can use his road car, and modifications (and thus expense) can be limited to essential safety requirements. One small point worth mentioning however, is that while our hero will certainly be racing, he most certainly will not be winning. It is a sad fact of life that in our present day would of commerically orientated motor sport, a production sports car will have to have a lot of money spent on it before being assured of success. In fact, although it would be logical to assume that *production* sports cars would be nowhere as expensive as *modified* sports cars, such is not the case. Just as in Production Saloon racing large sums of money need to be spent, first in buying the latest model, then in having it completely stripped and rebuilt taking full advantage of the regulations. This will have to be done by a professional race preparation specialist and the car will almost certainly need one or two rebuilds during the season.

Although still a young formula, Prod Sports has had its share of political unrest. Cars which complied with the exact letter of the regulations but not with the spirit of them, have been protested again and again to the scrutineers, but as nothing was found legally wrong they were naturally passed as being O.K. This caused discontent, but one can hardly blame the scrutineers. Or indeed the organisers. After all, if commercialism is introduced into a sport, and a driver is commercially sponsored, it is that driver's job to win races. And it is not just driving skill that wins races; it is a combination of skills in driving, in choosing the Class with the biggest potential, then picking a car with the biggest potential and preparing it to the fullest degree, while staying within the framework of the written regulations. Should the car then be so successful that it beats everyone else to the detriment of the racing in the eyes of the other competitors, then they should try to improve their own skills or, at the end of the year, lobby that the rules be changed for the following year. What they should NOT do is cry 'Mommy, I don't wanna play any more', when they find themselves being pushed down the results table during the year. However, that's just the authors opinion and no doubt many will differ.

Modified Sports Cars

This class of racing developed from the Freddie Dixon Marque Cars class which was so popular and successful in the '60s. It is a formula especially designed for the amateur racing driver and not primarily for spectators, although many of the races provide superb spectator value. Neither would it be of much interest to a motor manufacturer or dealer keen to promote his product, as it carries virtually no publicity.

There is a specified list of selected eligible cars, designed to suit the drivers, which includes suitable production cars and excludes anything outside the 'spirit' of the class. This is an R.A.C. approved formula and is the direct result of the combined views of the competitors, the B.A.R.C. and the B.R.S.C.C. who both run Championships for the cars throughout the season. In fact if one were to have the time and sufficient money it would be possible to run in both Championships in a total of almost thirty races.

The cars are familiar sports cars produced for road use and modified quite considerably to give real racing performance. The eligibility of cars and the class divisions vary year to year as new cars and different engines appear on the market, or when the drivers or the promoting clubs feel there is a need for a change. A few years ago many of the competitors drove their cars to the circuit, changed the plugs, and then went out and raced. A competitive car today is seldom a road machine however, but this is still a relatively cheap class of racing (it can be very much cheaper than Production Sports Cars, for example) and one thoroughly enjoyed by the drivers.

The following list is of cars eligible during 1976/77 shows the great variety of cars which can be raced. The list appears each year in the R.A.C. 'Blue Book' and is reviewed annually, but basically remains unaltered.

Eligible cars:
AC: Ace; Ace Bristol; Cobra 4.7.
Alfa Romeo: Giulia GTA, Spider, Sprint G.T., Sprint GTC, SS, 2600 Sprint, 2600 Spider GTV, Spider 1300, 1750 Spider Veloce, JZ 1300.
Arkley: SS.
Aston Martin: DB4, DB4GT, DB4GT Zagato, DB5GT, DB6, DB6 Series 2.
Austin Healey: 100 (all models), 100-six, 3000 (all models); all Sprites.
Caterham: Super 7.
Chevrolet: Sting Ray (not Grand Sport).
Clan: Crusader.
Daimler: SP250.
Datsun: 240Z, 260Z.
Davrian: Imp and Mini engines.
De Tomaso: Pantera.
Elva: Courier (all models).
Ferrari: 275 GTB, 275 GTS, 330 GT, Dino 246, +308, Daytona.
Gilbern: Invader.
Ginetta: G4, G15.
Honda: 600S, S800.
Jaguar: XK 120, 140, 150; E-type 3.8 and 4.2.
Jensen: Healey.
Lenham: Le Mans Coupe.
Lotus: Elite (Mk 1 and 2), Elan, Europa, Espirit.
MG: MGA, MGB, MGC, Midgets.
Marcos: Volvo 1800, Ford 1500/1600/V4 and 3 litre, Mini.
Mini: Jem.
Morgan: +4, 4/4, +8.
Piper: 1600cc.
Porsche: 911, 914, 914/6, Turbo.
Reliant: Scimitar GTE.

Shelby: Cobra 4.7.
Sunbeam: Tiger, Alpine.
Triumph: TR3, TR4, TR5, TR6, TR7, Spitfires, GT6, Stag.
Turner: 950, 998, 1080, 1500.
TVR: Grantura, 1800, Vixen, Tuscan.
Unipower: GT.

This extensive list comes to a massive total of well over 100 different model types from which the Mod Sports competitor can pick a car.

There are four different Classes in which to race, and these are the same for both the promoting Clubs Championships: up to 1100cc; 1151cc to 1500cc; 1501cc to 2000cc; and over 2000cc.

Politics has been refreshingly absent from Mod Sports, although the inclusion of Lotus 7s and Porsche 911 Carrera's which were faster than anything else in their Classes caused quite a bit of a furore in the early '70s. They were dropped from the list of eligible cars after a certain amount of agitation by their colleagues, and the series is now healthier than it has ever been.

Purists might think it a pity that such lovely old machinery such as a Jaguar XK, big Healey or an Aston Martin is chopped about by the fitting of wider wheel arches and cosmetic air-dams; but to be realistic, these cars are so expensive to maintain in Concours condition that if this was not done, they would probably just rust away through neglect.

So there it is; a formula very much for the amateur driver and with very few restrictions so that a competitor can approach it as lightly or as seriously as he wishes.

Thoroughbred Sports Cars

This category of Club racing was conceived by Anthony Hutton, Competition Secretary of the Jaguar Drivers Club, who with John Harper, a prominent driver in Club events, developed a keen interest not just in Jaguars but in other early post-war sports-cars. The cars they were interested in were the everyday sports-cars which were fairly common in the halcyon days when the choice was wide and the price required to buy something with a folding top was not anywhere near as high as it is now. Many of these cars were still just about road-worthy, but as the years went by they passed their M.O.T. tests with greater difficulty and Hutton and Harper reckoned that a series of races would give their owners a new incentive to get the cars going well again.

It was obviously going to be difficult in many cases to return the cars to their original condition, so it was decided that while the bodywork would visually have to remain basically the same as when the cars were built, the suspension could be modified slightly and the engine extensively.

An organisation called Forward Enterprises (now known as Speed Action Enterprises) was set up to administer the new formula, and the first race was run at Thruxton in 1972 and proved immensely popular with all who took part.

To qualify, cars need only be sports cars, manufactured between 1946 and 1959, and there was such a variety of suitable cars made in the late forties and fifties that anyone interested in Thoroughbred Sports Car racing should have no problem in being able to find a suitable example from the following list of eligible models:

AC (2 litres).
Aston Martin DB Marks 1; 2; 2/4; 4.
Austin Healey 100/4; 100/6; 3000.
M.G.A.
Morgan 4/4; +4.
Triumph TR2; 3; 3A.
Jaguar XK120; 140; 150.
Elva Courier (MGA engine).
Lotus Elite.

Porsche 356.
Healey Silverstone.
Fraser Nash.

There are three Classes catered for: up to 1600cc; from 1600 to 2700cc and from 2700cc upwards.

There is a Championship in which the cars can compete consisting of some eight races throughout the season and details of the Championship and the cars can be had from: Speed Action Enterprises, 29 Lennox Gardens, London S.W.1.

The Thoroughbred Sports Car category of racing is another of those categories of racing which ensures that just about everyone can get a race at some time or some place in whatever sort of car might take his fancy, in British Club racing. It is not by any means expensive, but as time goes by it will probably become increasingly difficult to find cars in good enough condition to race without having to spend a prohibitive amount of money in order to restore them to good running order. However, the formula was started by enthusiasts and continues to be run by enthusiasts purely for enthusiasts, and so probably has as good if not a better chance of continuing to flourish than some better promoted formulae started for purely commerical reasons.

Historic Sports Cars

The Historic Sports Car Club was founded at the end of 1965 by members of the Frazer Nash Car Club. Their objective was to preserve, and provide races for, the historic Sport-scars and Sports-Touring cars of special quality which had been produced in the years after the second World War. Many of these cars had been decaying either because of age or lack of use, while a lot of the better British built examples were being exported just to be rebuilt and stored in museums overseas.

The founder committee of the Club felt that if they could run a series of races specifically for these cars, owners' interest would be revived and many examples which might have otherwise disappeared for ever would be saved.

For the first three years after the founding of the Club, Historic cars ran under the banner of the Frazer Nash Club, but they got full recognition from the R.A.C. in 1969 and in that year the official Historic Sports Car Club ran its first race in which some 25 entries started, at Castle Combe in Wiltshire.

The Club has divided the post-war cars in to five main Classes:

Group 1; Historic: 1940 to 1959. Sports and Sports Racing cars of special quality, produced in small numbers.

Group 2; Post Historic: 1960 to 1964. Sports and Sports Racing cars used in International competition, of which not more than 500 had been built.

Group 3; Historic Production cars: Sports cars, of which more than 500 were made or imported; over twelve years old and out of production for more than 7 years.

Group 4; From 1965; Sports and Sports Racing cars, less than 500 of which were made or imported; over 7 years old and which were used in International competition.

Single Seaters: 1940 to 1961. Formula 1 or 2 racing cars; front or rear engines.

The great difference between Historic Sports Car Racing and other equally specialised types of racing such as Thoroughbred Sports Cars, is that the Historic Sports Car Club's main stipulation is that the cars should be completely original both in bodywork and mechanically. They have managed to achieve this aim with a remarkable degree of success and the Club are now the considered experts on post-war Sports Cars.

Some of the cars which have appeared in the Clubs races have included Ferrari 275 LM's; Jaguar D-types; Maserati's; Lister Jaguars and Lister Chevrolets; Lotus 11's; the ex-Le Mans Aston Martin P212; Coopers; Lotus Elans and Elites; Lightweight Jaguar E-types; and Connaughts, etc.

The cars are almost all highly specialised, beautifully prepared and maintained, and are usually driven with reliability and care rather than speed. But nonetheless they provide a stirring spectacle for those of us who didn't see them in their hey-day and they are immensely popular with the more knowledgeable spectators. Many of the revived models are now worth far more than when they were bought originally, which is a pity in a way, as this means that the owners tend to grow less and less keen to race them as their value increases.

Historic Sports Cars racing is the ideal let-out for any enthusiast who has a car which falls into one of the Clubs' categories and who doesn't want to see it just sit at home in premature retirement. It is also an ideal formula for the driver who wants to enjoy his racing without being involved every weekend, and who, with a bit of luck, can look forward to his car appreciating in value rather than depreciating, whether he races it or not.

Vintage Sports Cars

Founded in 1934 the Vintage Sports Car Club was originally formed to cater for the owners of cars built before January 1st, 1931. The sphere of its activity is now much wider and as well as running all manner of social meetings, film-shows and the like, it organises some sixteen competitive events during the year for owners of exotic machinery not just from before 1931, but from quite a few years later.

Eligible cars are now classified into four main periods:

1. Edwardian: Cars manufactured on or before 31st Dec. 1918.

2. Vintage: Cars manufactured on or before 31st Dec. 1930.

3. Post-vintage Thoroughbred: Cars manufactured on or before 31st Dec. 1940 and accepted by the committee as eligible.

4. Historic Racing Cars; Cars specially built for racing

or cars specially modified and raced in any of the following sub-periods:

Group 1. Racing cars of a type which competed in races or speed events on or before 31st Dec. 1943.

Group 2. Single seater racing cars of 4 or more cylinders built between 1st Jan. 1944 and 31st Dec 1953.

Group 3. Front engined Grand Prix cars which competed in Formula 1 races in 1954 to 1960.

Group 4. Single-seater front engined cars of historical importance or particular interest.

Group 5. Sports cars raced in international events before 31st Dec. 1943.

There are further sub-divisions of eligible cars into types:

(a) Vintage Racing cars: Cars of a type raced on or before 31st Dec. 1930 and accepted as such by the committee.

(b) Modified Cars: The broad rule is that only modifications which could have been done at the time of the cars' period, plus certain specified modifications, are allowed.

(c) Modified Sports Cars: Similar to above, and must be suitable for use on the road.

(d) Standard Sports Cars: These must have been catalogued as Sports Cars by their makers and must be basically unchanged, with certain specified exceptions.

(e) Touring Cars: Similar to (d) above.

(f) Light cars: Vintage cars of not more than 30 horse power.

These are only the general classifications of the cars; the rules and requirements and permitted modifications run into several pages and while it is relatively easy to become a member of the V.S.C.C., before entering one of their events it will be necessary to make sure that the car will pass eligibility scrutineering.

The Vintage Sports Car Club is probably the most exclusive in Britaish Club racing. The machinery produced at their rare but not to be missed meetings is unique, expensive and irreplaceable. The following is just a short list of some of the more exotic examples which have regularly appeared at their races: Alvis; Bentley; Invicta; Bugatti; Lea Francis; Amilcar; G.N; Talbot; Bentley Royce; Lagonda; Hotchkiss; H.R.G.; E.R.A.; Salmson; Straker Squire; Bentley Napier; Barnato Hassan Special and Hutton Delage.

The majority of the drivers compete for the fun of it rather than with any hope of winning anything, although it is not unknown for equally matched cars to get so carried away that they begin putting in laps at around the same times that their cars set when they were brand new! More than one such "race within a race" has ended in tears, with the sad owner surveying the remains of his pride and joy piled into the sleepers on the outside of Woodcote at Silverstone.

To most British Club drivers, the race is the thing rather than the cars they drive, but in the V.S.C.C. this is seldom, if ever, the case. The cars themselves are the main interest and the racing a showcase where they can be displayed and compared. Cars change hands for amounts of money unheard of in other branches of Club racing—figures in the region of £15,000 are not unheard of—and they are expensive to maintain if they are raced regularly. They are extremely expensive to maintain if they are raced and crashed regularly.

To sum up; the Vintage Sports Cars, or any of the other cars which the Club caters for, are a superb hobby for the man who wishes to cherish a 'golden olden' car and compete with it occasionally, provided of course, that he can afford it. The mention of the odd damaging crash should not put one off racing an old car as the Club is carefull to 'seed' entries whenever possible into similar performance groups, and the style of driving is gentlemenly in the extreme. Also no matter how slow or how old one's car, there will always be a place for it in events provided it is eligible. Many of the races too, are run to a handicap so it is possible that even the slowest car might come away from a meeting with at least an honorary award.

Formula Four

It was through Alan Burgess, one of the leading lights in Drag racing when that sport was introduced to Great Britain in the early sixties, that the author had his first contact with Formula 4. Burgess had imported what must have been the first example of the formula from Italy, intending it to be a step between the spectacular and very fast 250cc Karts of the time and proper motor racing. Looking for all the world like a scaled-down Formula 3 car, but with only a 250cc engine, the cars unfortunately never really caught on in their original form. A change was made after a few abortive seasons to 650cc engines, but these too proved unsuitable and the cars were generally lacking both in spectacle and in reliability. With its small original engine the car was meant to be a 'grown-up' kart with racing car bodywork, but as the engine sizes got bigger it became more of a scaled-down Formula Ford and lost all connection with its karting background. After several years in the doldrums, in the early seventies the ubiquitous Seven Fifty Motor Club adopted Formula 4 and since then the popularity of the little single seater, rear engined racing cars has increased in leaps and bounds.

Car . . . there are no real restrictions governing chassis design other than the normal R.A.C. Vehicle Regulations. These are available from the Motor Sport Division in Belgrave Square, London.

Bodywork. . . . The cars must be single seat racing cars with rear mounted engines. Aerodynamic devices, i.e. wings and spoilers are permitted in conformity with Formula 3 regulations. These are defined in the F.I.A. year book. It must be possible for the driver to enter and leave the car without removing any part of the chassis or body work. Fuel tanks can be either metal or bag type, but, if metal, must be covered in fire proof R.A.C. approved material. The cars must be equipped with a dual braking system so that in the case of failure in one system, braking will be retained on either both front or both rear wheels. An effective roll-over bar must be fitted which must be at least 5cm higher than the top of the driver's helmet when he is seated in the car.

Engine. . . . Maximum permitted capacity of the engine is 1000cc. It must be of British manufacture, either Ford, B.L.M.C. or Chrysler U.K. Although the standard basic engine components must be retained, plenty of scope is given for modification to increase power output. Fuel injection is not permitted and neither is supercharging. Chrysler and B.L.M.C. engines are allowed freedom of carburettor choice both in size and number of chokes, but Ford engine carburettors must be fitted with a carburettor restrictor.

Transmission. . . . Choice of gearbox is free but only four forward gears are permitted. Reverse gear must also be fitted and must be operational.

There are no restrictions on wheels and tyres.

It will be seen from the above extracts from the regulations governing Formula 4 that both the R.A.C. and the 750 M.C. are quite happy to keep restrictions to a minimum. Most of the regulations are aimed at promoting safety, and the 750 club considers that the 1000cc upper limit governs potential performance quite effectively, without invoking complex restrictions on choice of tyres, aerodynamic aids, and the like.

Yet, although restricted to being the smallest engine size in single seater racing, the cars are still incredibly quick and in the 1976 season the faster cars were lapping the Brands Hatch Club circuit at 88 m.p.h., which is quicker than Formula Ford. Indeed at Mallory Park in 1974 the first 100 m.p.h., Formula 4 lap was set.

The Formula has not had much success in obtaining overall sponsorship for its National Championship, but in spite of this lack of commercialism, or perhaps because of it, the number of competitors continues to increase, making for full grids on all but a few occasions.

It is interesting to note that competitors in Formula 4, as in the other 750 M.C., formulae, are expected to behave in a responsible manner and the club actually state in their rules that a high standard of preparation is essential and will be insisted upon by the scrutineers before the cars are allowed on to the track at any of their meetings.

While new car prices are rather more expensive than one might have thought, and are creeping towards £4,000, the *Autosport* Market Place usually manages to turn up second-hand examples for less than £2,000. But perhaps the best source of specific information on either new or second-hand cars, or indeed anything at all to do with the Formula is the 750 M.C., itself.

The formula is increasing in popularity year by year, and in the 1975 Championship, run by the 750 Club, no less than forty different competitors started in a total of twenty races during the season. The racing is close and as we have seen, remarkably quick, and although the little cars might not warrant the attention of drivers aspiring to ultimate professionalism, any club driver or newcomer to the sport just interested in single seater racing for the sheer enjoyment of it, could do far worse than pick Formula 4.

The Monoposto Formula

The monoposto, or single-seater, class of racing had its beginnings like, so many others, in the early days of the ubiquitous 750 Motor Club.

Back in the mid '50s the Club had as its two racing formulae, the Austin 7 based 750 class and the Ford 1172 based slightly more powerful class. Both of these were basically two-seater, home built specials and were attracting an increasing number of devotees who were looking for low cost motor racing. However, in spite of the success of both

11 A35's, Morris Minors, Zephyr/Zodiac, Borgward, Lancias and numerous Jaguars showing the great variety in Classic Car racing

12 *above* Trevor Scarborough tests the Armco barriers at Rufforth during a round of the BRSCC run Ford Escort Challenge

13 *below* A Centaur, a DNC and an Arcos in a Reliant 750 Championship round at Lydden Hill

14 *above* Typical Club drivers during a general practice day at Silverstone. While Martin Moorhead, one of the leading Mini 850 men, files down a new set of brake drums to try to make them fit his wheels, Dave Elmer despairs of getting his Reliant 750 to start, let alone stop. The author's wife and her motor racing dog look on

15 *below* Alan Webb and Malcolm Jackson racing Clubmans cars at Silverstone

16 *above* Motor Racing is expensive. The Monoposto Brabham BT21C of Paul Maxwell after a Paddock bend shunt at Brands Hatch in June 1976. Note the fuel injection, large rear wing, fragile looking, but presumably strong enough, roll-over bar, prominent Goodyear sticker on the cockpit top and Firestone tyre fitted to the rear!

17 *below* A Lotus Elan and a Clan lead a Modified Sports car field at Longridge

18 *below* Well-modified E types in a Modsports race at Oulton Park

19 *above* A Monopost starting grid at Brands Hatch. Restrictions are few in this class of racing and many and varied are the different aerodynamic aids, wheel and tyre sizes and engine modifications which appear

20 *below* The 1976 Formula 3 Hawke designed by Adrian Reynard

21 *above* A Formula Super Vee and a Formula Four seen as part of a display organised by the B.A.R.C. in the Paddock at Brands Hatch during the 1976 British Grand Prix. Formula 1 cars they are not, but even though their appeal is limited in Club racing, at least they *look* like proper racing cars

22 *below* Tiga Formula Ford rear end. Note the megaphone type exhaust, huge oil tank and catch tank, tail light, Hewland engine and gearbox and the detailed finish of major components

23 A Formula Ford Tiga. Built and created by the combined brains of Howden Ganley and Tim Schenken, racing drivers both, the cars are superbly made and, certainly in 1976, the most expensive to buy of these formulae, there were a few of the members of the 750 Club who were not really content with two seater racing and who wanted to get into 'real' racing cars i.e. single seater ones, but without having to invest the great amounts of money that this style of racing normally involves. Frank Tiedeman, an Estate Agent from West London, was one of these.

Tiedeman had been a member of the Club for some time and had built and raced his own 750 Special with some degree of success. He also built, and raced, the first rear-engined car in the Ford 1172 Class. But Tiedeman was not too happy at having to build his cars to the limitations of the 750 Clubs formulae and as a result of a certain amount of agitation by him, both in the Club membership and in the correspondence columns of the leading motoring magazines of the time, he began to stimulate a lot of interest in the formation of a new class of amateur motor racing specifically for single seaters. His main argument was that it seemed a little silly to build and race cars ostensibly as two seaters, and he claimed there was a growing need for low cost motor racing without any of the accoutrements which went with the little 750 and 1172 cars, such as wings, headlights, passenger seats, spare wheels etc.

In the magazine *Motor Sport*, Denis Jenkinson wrote an article commending Tiedemans ideas and this was backed by John Bolster in the weekly *Autosport*. Both of these well known journalists carried a lot of weight, then as now, and the added credence that they gave to Tiedemans ideas brought sufficient interest to warrant the formation in 1958 of the Monoposto Register. Both Jenkinson and Bolster showed they had the courage of their convictions by becoming founder members. Soon there were sufficient competitors with suitable machines to run the first race, and this was held at Brands Hatch where Tiedeman himself finished second using his old 1172 car stripped of all surplus extras.

Meanwhile, back at the 750 Club, some of the members

had begun to feel a little peeved at the departure of several of their active colleagues and they felt that the single seater brigade would detract from their own two existing formulae Tiedeman however insisted that all three formulae could exist side by side and not only did he not desert his old Club, he even became a member of the Board and at one time Chairman.

Inevitably though, as time went by and the new formula became more and more popular, an ever increasing number of low cost, home-built single seaters began to put in an appearance, the gap between the two lots of enthusiasts widened and finally the Monoposto section section split completely from the parent Club and in 1965 became fully independent.

In its formative years the Monoposto Club had as its mainstay not so much pure single seaters as 1172 Class two seaters stripped of the extras that the 750 Clubs 1172 Formula had demanded. The maximum engine capacity was kept to 1200cc but apart from this, restrictions in the regulations were kept to a minimum.

Naturally single seater builders were encouraged and soon the starting grids of races run to the Monoposto Formula began to look more and more like Formula 2 or even Formula 1 grids, even though the cars were smaller.

As time went by the Formula retained the original basic format of cheap single seater racing, but periodical changes were introduced in order to keep interest and support alive and active. At the beginning of the '60s Ford brought out the Anglia 997cc over square engine, and this proved to be an ideal substitute for the by then out-dated and hard to find 1172 unit. Soon after that, instead of continuing with the one 1200cc limit class, the racers were divided into two separate classes; Class A with an upper capacity limit of 1200cc and Class B with an upper limit of 1500cc. The upper limit changed to 1600cc in time and in the early '70s the lower limit was dropped due to lack of support.

Not all of the cars raced are home built. When the old

Italian inspired Formula Junior racing finished in Great Britain in the early '60s, a lot of the cars were left lying around and to all intents and purposes were obsolete as far as circuit racing was concerned. Their owners prevailed upon the Monoposto Club to allow them to take part in the ever increasing number of races for the Club's home built cars, and their 1100cc engines made them roughly competitive with the larger capacity of the Specials. At first, when the proprietary built cars were allowed into Monoposto racing, it was felt that this might detract from the principles on which it was formed, but this was found not to be the case and over the years there has been a pretty good balance between the two types of car.

At the present time both the home built cars and the 'bought-in' ones are limited to an upper capacity limit of 1600cc, but the professionally built racers are regulated to trail behind the home-built ones in vintage by five or six years. During the 1976 season for example no proprietary cars built later than September 1970 were allowed, but though this might sound limiting no less than 37 different models from some 19 manufacturers could legally have been used.

It is rather a pity in a way that proprietary built cars, no matter what their vintage, are used in Monoposto racing but at least they don't run away with all the prizes. Indeed, it says a lot for the ingenuity of the Clubs constructor members when it is realised that their own cars are often every bit as fast, and sometimes faster, than the genuine factory jobs.

The Club is run very much for enthusiasts and any form of over-active commercialism is frowned upon. Advertising on the cars is strictly controlled and is restricted to products actually in use on the cars, or fitted to them. Drivers must enter races under their own names and works or sponsored entries are expressly excluded. The Club run their own year long championship and again this is run 'for the love of it', and there are no monetary rewards for any of the races or even for the overall championship.

Technically, the regulations governing Monoposto stipulate that the cars are single seater racing cars with all four wheels fully exposed and with either front or rear mounted engines. Engines are limited to an upper capacity of 1600cc and must be push-rod operated. Superchargers are not allowed. Starter motors, fire extinguishers and rear lights are not compulsory but are recommended. Advertising decals on the cars are limited to eight pairs, each no larger than 55 square inches, provided they apply to products used on or fitted to the car.

To discourage professionalism one of the Club rules states that it is forbidden to have cars built, prepared or maintained professionally. This last rule is obviously quite difficult to enforce and on the thankfully rare occasions when cheating has taken place, or at least when it has been found to have taken place, it has invariably been because some over enthusiastic competitor has allowed his money to run away with his brains.

Monoposto racing has come a long way since Frank Tiedeman and his chums first conceived the idea of low cost single-seater racing. It is no longer inexpensive, it is for example about three times more expensive to race a successful Monoposto than a successful 750, but it is still the cheapest way to go motor racing with a single seater. There is a good feeling of camaraderie in the Club (every driver must become a member) and the number of active competition members is now creeping towards 100. Membership is mainly confined to Great Britain and the formula is very much a National one.

Monoposto racing would have very little appeal for the aspiring professional and almost none for the Club racer wanting primarily a low cost form of motor racing, but it has its own place in the world of British Club racing and without it many of the older Formula Fords, Formula 2's and Formula 3's would have long since disappeared from the circuits.

Formula Ford 1600

'Single seater racing cars fitted with a standard push-rod Cortina G.T. engine and with open coachwork.' For over ten years this simple quote, taken from the R.A.C. year book, has described what is probably the most popular single seater racing car formula in Great Britain.

Originally conceived and developed by Motor Racing Stables at Brands Hatch as training vehicles for their pupils, the cars were so obviously suitable as pure racing cars in their own right, that with the combined backing of Grovewood Securities, who own four of the countries major racing circuits, and the Ford Motor Company, a new racing formula was soon born. The new formula was intended basically to provide a cheaper form of single seater racing than Formula 3 and although prices have virtually trebled in the intervening years, it still conforms in principle to the original ideals.

By using space-frame construction, that is to say a tubular chassis with detachable body panels, instead of the more expensive monocoque construction of Formula 3 and sometimes Formula Super Vee, Formula Ford deliberately attracted the smaller constructors and private teams and discouraged the designers of the faster formulae. This limiting of chassis design coupled with the use of basically standard Ford engines has contributed more than anything else to keeping the costs relatively low. Indeed it is still possible to be amongst the leaders in a Formula Ford race using a chassis of several years vintage, and thus the Formula achieves another of its original aims, which was to promote driver ability rather than design/constructor ability.

The Formula is a superb training ground for single seater racing drivers and is the obvious first step of the ladder to a Formula 1 drive. Emmerson Fitippaldi, James Hunt, Tom Pryce and Jody Scheckter and many others all graduated from Formula Ford. It is also regarded as an end in itself by many who are quite happy to compete season after season in the myriad Championships open to them in Great Britain and on the Continent.

In 1976 there were over half a dozen different Championships for the Formula, ranging from the six-round R.A.C. Championship to the twenty-round Championships of D.J.M. Records and Townsend Thorenson Ferries. So it can be seen that there is no shortage of races up and down the country throughout the season, but this is not to say that a driver shouldn't get his entries in quickly, as the grids are almost always full, and the reserve list invariably over-subscribed.

Wings and aerodynamic aids have always been prohibited and the only major change in the rules came in 1975 when racing tyres were allowed for the first time. Up to then it had been hoped that by using road tyres costs would be kept down, but in fact the wheel-to-wheel battles of the furiously driving Formula Ford pilots consumed these tyres at an alarming rate and a decision was made to change.

Unfortunately, however, all has not been sweetness and light in the formula and over the years it has gained notoriety for bad driving, political wranglings, scrutineering disqualifications *ad nauseam,* flagrant cheating and downright bad sportsmanship which one supposes in a way contributes to its suitability as a would-be professional's training ground, but is to be deplored nonetheless. A planned programme of rule tightening and more rigid scrutineering together with severer penalties for cases of bad driving, have done a lot to ease these problems in recent years, and it is to be hoped that the formula will soon achieve the total respect that it so richly deserves.

For newcomers an ideal start would be a course or lessons at one of the recognised racing driver schools, as these schools all use Formula Ford racing cars as training vehicles. There the new driver can satisfy himself as to his ability, and gain invaluable experience on the track without involving himself in the considerable cost of first buying a single seater car of his own. Indeed, it is not necessary even to go to the expense of a full training course as most of the schools will allow a driver to sample a car in the form of an introductory lesson, for several laps, albeit at reduced revs, for a cost of not much more than £20.

Some of the schools run schemes whereby the more promising students take part in races against other pupils and the more successful are, on occasion, actually offered a sponsored car for selected races or even for a full season. Should a pupil not achieve a school sponsored drive, then at least he will have a recommendation from the school that he has completed their course and this will help him in future sponsorship deals, or in negotiations with manufacturers from whom he might wish to buy a car. It is often the case that a driver with a good starting record can negotiate a discount on a new car price with the manufacturer, or perhaps the purchase of spares at a discount in return for the manufacturer using him for public relations/advertising. This is known as a semi (sometimes very semi) 'works' drive.

In Formula Ford as in every other form of racing, costs have risen alarmingly in recent years. At the end of the sixties a new Formula Ford top class car with winning potential would cost £1,500 and a really good second-hand car would cost about £1,200. Sadly these days are long gone and now, or at least at the time of writing, a new rolling chassis, that is to say a complete car but without an engine, will cost around £2,500, while second-hand cars, also without an engine, will cost around £1,600. Although modifications to Formula Ford engines are strictly limited, and essentially only blue printing and balancing is allowed, a professionally built engine will still cost around £600, and a driver can reckon on possibly two engine rebuilds during the season at around £200 a time.

This then is Formula Ford. Immensely popular with race organisers, drivers and spectators, it has gained in stature over the years and there is every reason to believe that it will continue to be the most popular form of single seater racing for many years to come. Motor racing is not cheap and never will be. Equipment, maintenance and repairs all contribute to making it one of the most expensive of all sports, but at least in Formula Ford a genuine attempt is being continually made to keep the formula specifications, and thus costs, at a level that will continue to make it the most viable single seater formula for the serious racing driver.

Formula Ford 2000

During the early '70s FF1600 had become so popular throughout the country that with two or even three events for the formula at most race meetings, there were still disappointed drivers whose entries were being turned down. Peter Browning, executive director of the B.R.S.C.C., again approached Motor Circuit Development's (previously Grovewood Securities) boss John Webb and the Ford Motor Company's director of motor sport for Europe, Stuart Turner, with his ideas for a possible solution. Between them it was decided to initiate a higher grade of Formula Ford racing which would provide a logical step between Formula Ford and Formula 3. This was designed to attract the cream of the existing Formula Ford drivers, and thus relieve the pressure on the 1600 grids.

Although the new cars would obviously be expensive it was decided to hold costs down as far as possible by retaining many of the original ideas of Formula Ford 1600. Thus the tubular construction chassis was retained and the engine was to be a standard Ford production unit. The choice of engine turned out to be pretty obvious as at that time the single overhead camshaft 2-litre Ford 'Pinto' engine, as used in the Escort RS 2000 and Cortina G.T., had already been seen in highly modified form in Formula 3 and Formula 2 and had stood up well to the rigours of racing. However, for the new Formula the engine was to be kept in standard form, with balancing and blue printing again the primary methods by which power out-put might be increased. The most obvious change on the new cars was the introduction of wings. These made them look quite 'grown-up' and while the more honest of the drivers were reluctantly to admit that these were of doubtful advantage, except possibly on the twistiest of circuits, at least they gave the budding aerodynamicists something to practice their skills upon.

Most of the regular Formula Ford manufacturers soon produced cars for the new class, although mainly these were adapted forms of existing Formula Ford 1600 design. Similarly most of the regular Formula Ford 1600 engine builders were soon offering 2000 units, and as a result of meetings between the engine builders and the R.A.C., to iron out any ambiguities in the engine regulations, before the Formula was publicly launched, Formula 2000 has been refreshingly free of protests.

During its first full season the cars seemed a little under-powered and this led to a relaxation of the R.A.C.'s stringent carburettor restrictions, resulting in a useful increase in power and bringing the B.H.P., output close to 130.

Although the formula was designed to keep costs as low as possible, it is still quite a bit more expensive than its more junior formula, and an engine-less rolling chassis will cost in the region of £3,200; an engine of proprietary build will cost around £700, but it should be possible to pick up a complete car with some spares from the advertisements in the back of *Autosport* for around £2,600. These prices, are naturally, at the time of writing.

Therefore it will be seen that during 1976/77 at least, the cost of a new car with engine and all running gear ready to drive would be in the region of £4,000, and a serious driver will almost certainly have at least one spare engine and will have to spend out close on £200 per rebuild during the season. It should be possible to do a season of some twenty races including practice sessions, on say, 2 sets of 'dry' racing tyres and two sets of 'wet' racing tyres, and these will cost around £250 for each set of four, complete with wheels. As we said before, motor racing is not cheap.

Originally it was suggested that to be eligible for the new Formula, drivers had to hold an International licence and had to have previous experience of single seater racing, and once having competed in FF2000, drivers were not to be allowed back to FF1600. However, these ideas were dropped very quickly, and now the only qualifications needed are the basic competition licence, and of course a healthy bank balance.

At the beginning, FF2000 attracted quite small fields but as more cars came on to the market for the new formula, and as drivers began making suitable sponsorship deals, the grids began to fill up. The bigger fields brought some excellent racing but although there were very few scrutineering and regulation infringements, the formula produced some rough-and-tumble driving. Crashes, when they happened, tended to be both spectacular and decimating and involved invariably more than one car. Indeed, at times almost half the entries were eliminated and many of the races had to be stopped and re-started. Speeds increased too quite appreciably during the first year of the formula, and towards the end of the season, the lap times of the faster cars were often four to five seconds quicker than at the beginning.

The formula is still basically a national one and perhaps when it becomes more international and when championships are run throughout Europe it will become more popular with the would-be professionals, as a club racing 'finishing school' and also as a talent spotting ground for the team managers from Formula 2 and Formula 1.

Although FF2000 on the face of it looks like a logical step for any driver on his way from FF1600 to greater things, there are some who would baulk at the enforced delay of perhaps a full season and would opt for jumping straight into Formula 3. Others, not quite ready for the big step into

Formula 3 may well decide to stay in FF1600 for an extra season and try to improve themselves in that Formula, rather than spend a transitory year in the more expensive and more commercial hurly-burly of FF2000. Perhaps the best thing that can be said about FF2000 is that it is faster than FF1600, thus making it the fastest single seater formula in club racing; assuming, if we do, that the phenomenal costs of Formula 3 take that particular Formula outside the sphere of the normal club driver.

It may well be that as the formula becomes more established it may very well attract newcomers, not primarily from slower formulae, but from Formula 3, where drivers not intending to go on to Formula 2 or Formula 1, might become increasingly disenchanted with their enormous costs.

Formula Vee and Super Vee

Although in essence a very logical form of single seater racing, using as it does, not just the engine, but the gearbox and many suspension and other component parts from its parent car (The Volkswagen Beetle) unlike Formula Ford which uses only the Ford engine, Formula Vee has never really caught on in Great Britain. It is hugely popular in the United States and to a lesser, but none-the-less wide-spread, extent in Europe, but in Britain it has always been overshadowed by Formula Ford. The main reason for this being that the Ford Formula has the backing of the British Ford Company who are manufacturers within the country, whereas Volkswagen G.B., are merely importers.

Begun in the early sixties in the West coast of American, Formula Vee spread quickly through the United States and later to Europe, where it prospered mainly as a result of financial backing from the Volkswagen parent factory in Germany. The formula increased in popularity, still based on the Volkswagen Beetle 1300, until in 1970, without wishing to discontinue the basic formula but wanting to increase performance the Americans, began to use the more powerful Volkswagen 1600cc engine and thus was born Formula Super Vee.

The two formulae were designed to run in parallel but in Europe at least, Super Vee has become the more popular and in Great Britain almost no new Formula Vee cars are being made, and it is likely that soon Formula Vee will be dropped altogether. Strangely enough, although the Formula is not as well supported in Great Britain as might have been hoped, there are more Super Vee constructors in this country than there are in the rest of the world combined. Indeed Volkswagen G.B., themselves export a vast amount of spares for Super Vee each year, and possibly for this reason support the Formula actively.

General description. . . . Both formula are designed for single seater racing cars based on original Volkswagen components. All Volkswagen parts used must be in the Volkswagen factory spare parts catalogue and/or carry a clear identification mark as original Volkswagen components, and must have undergone all the parent factory working processes during manufacture. Other equipment and components are permitted only if contained in the full detailed regulations which are available from the British Formula Vee Association. Additional adaptation work is permitted to the standard components provided it is possible at all times to establish that they are standard production parts.

Minimum weight without fuel and driver is 375 kg for Vee and 400 kg for Super Vee. Both formulae have basically the same chassis and body work restrictions, the main difference being that wings and aerofoils are allowed in Super Vee but not in Vee.

In Formula Vee the front axle must be an original from a 1300 Beetle retaining the trailing arm torsion bar design. In Super Vee the design of the front suspension is unrestricted but Volkswagen stub axles, wheel hubs, brake discs and brake calpiers must be used. The rear axle and suspension design in Formula Vee must be of trailing link construction with coil springs. In Formula Super Vee rear suspension design is unrestricted, except that Volkswagen half shafts, universal joints, wheel hubs and some brake parts must be used.

The bodywork design in both Formulae can either be monocoque or tubular frame, although in Great Britain, at least, monocoque examples are rare.

The 1300cc and 1600cc engines in both formulae must be built from standard Volkswagen parts, or where these are permitted to be changed, the replacement parts must be to Volkswagen dimensions, and super charging is not allowed.

Volkswagen gearboxes are compulsory in both formulae. Since the beginning of 1976 both formulae have been permitted to use racing tyres.

To compete in either Formula Vee or Super Vee National Championships, it is necessary to be a member of the Formula Vee Association of Great Britain which is based at Volkswagen House in Purley in Surrey. The Association keeps in constant touch with its members and issues many useful club bulletins and technical papers, all designed to help their members. The Association also periodically circulates a very useful price list of second-hand cars, and this is of great help to someone considering racing either of the Vee Formula, as some of the cars on offer can be bought at remarkably low prices. Indeed at the time of writing should one find the close on £6,000 price of a new Super Vee prohibitive, before dismissing the Formula completely it might be worth looking at some of the second-hand Vee cars on offer for less than £1,000 or second-hand Super Vees at around £3,000. The second-hand Super Vee cars are generally to latest specifications and quite competitive. Certainly you cannot expect to be up amongst the leaders, but at least you'll be racing.

One of the most successful engine builders is Heidegger of Switzerland who charge around £1,300 for a Formula Vee engine and around £1,800 for a Formula Super Vee engine. Both engines are built to latest specifications and ready to race. The prices are ex-London and further information on Heidegger can be had from the Formula Vee Association.

In future it is more than likely that the water cooled 1600cc Volkswagen engine and possibly the 2000cc engine will soon make their appearance in Super Vee. These will naturally give the cars a further increase in performance and may just revive some of the flagging interest in the Formula nationally.

At first glance this class of racing might not seem an ideal choice for the British club driver. There are only some thirty Super Vee cars in total, actively competing in the whole of Great Britain, and races seldom attract more than fifteen starters. However, should a driver be considering venturing into Europe, where the real prestige and prize money is to be found, then the Formula would be much more attractive and viewed in this context the fewer number of races at home and the £5,500 average price for a new Super Vee might not be such an off-putting consideration.

Circuit Guide

Motor racing has become so popular that there are now no less than 16 circuits throughout Great Britain.
These are, in alphabetical order:-

AINTREE
BRANDS HATCH
CADWELL PARK
CASTLE COOMBE
CROFT
INGLISTON
KNOCKHILL
LLANDOW
LONGRIDGE
LYDDEN
MALLORY PARK
OULTON PARK
RUFFORTH
SILVERSTONE
SNETTERTON
THRUXTON

AINTREE

Situation: 5 miles North East of Liverpool, accessible from the Melling Road, by Blue Anchor Bridge. It is about a mile off the M57 motorway, which itself ties in with other motorways.

Address: Aintree Circuit, Liverpool. Or Aintree Circuit Club, 63 Andover Crescent, Tan House Farm, Winstanley, Wigan. Telephone: Wigan 213275.

Circuit Length: 1.64 miles.

General Practice: Club practice days organised by Aintree Circuit Club on Tuesdays between April and September. Details from the club.

Now a Club circuit, awaiting the decision on the future of the famous Grand Nation N.H. race and the development of the site, which means that there is uncertainty about the future. The result is that investment in full facilities has not taken place and there are very few permanent amenities for spectators. Best viewing is between the start and the two following corners, County Corner and Village Corner.

Aintree used to be a full International Circuit and it was here that Stirling Moss broke the stranglehold of the Italians on Grand Prix racing by winning the British Grand Prix in his Vanwall on July 20th 1957.

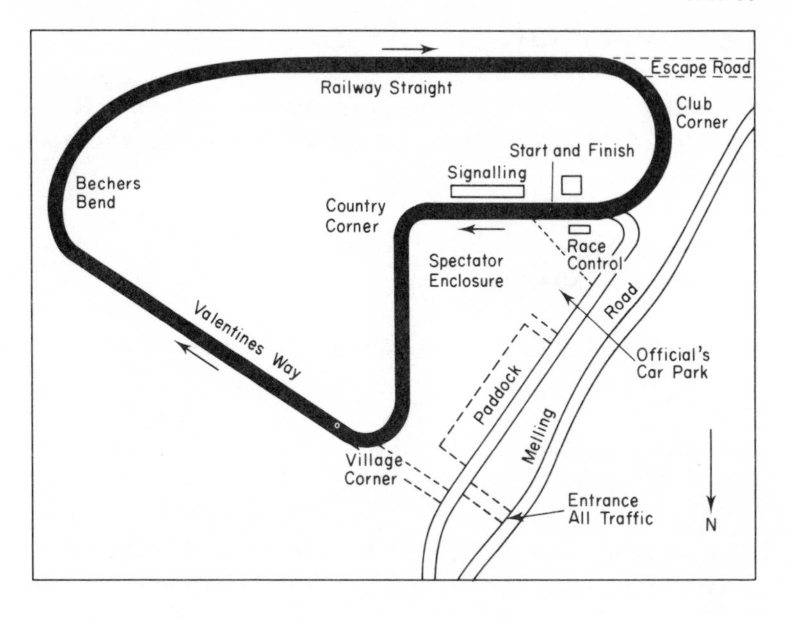
Escape Road
Railway Straight
Club
Corner
Start and Finish
Signalling
Bechers
Bend
Country
Corner
Race
Control
Spectator
Enclosure
Road
Valentines Way
Official's
Car Park
Paddock
Melling
Village
Corner
Entrance
All Traffic
N

BRANDS HATCH

Situation: South East of London near Farningham in Kent, on the London to Maidstone road. By car it takes about an hour from London.

Address: Brands Hatch Circuit Ltd., Fawkham, Kent. Telephone: Ash Green 872331.

Circuit Length: Grand Prix circuit 2.6 miles; Club circuit 1.24 miles.

General Practice: Wednesday and Saturday. Check by telephone first.

The most famous and arguably the best, motor racing circuit in the country. For spectators the viewing is superb, especially when just the Club circuit is being used and before the new pits complex was built in 1976, the whole of the short circuit could be seen from several track side viewing points. For drivers, both circuits combine straights, fast and slow corners and a hairpin into one immensely satisfying experience. Paddock Bend with its blind flat-out approach and fast downhill exit is particularly demanding.

There are plenty of cafe facilities and bars but, as at the majority of British circuits these can be very poor; far better to bring a hamper. There is a good pub near-by, the Lion Hotel in Farningham, with pleasant lawns by a river.

Brands Hatch is the home of Motor Racing Stables who have been there for something like fifteen years.

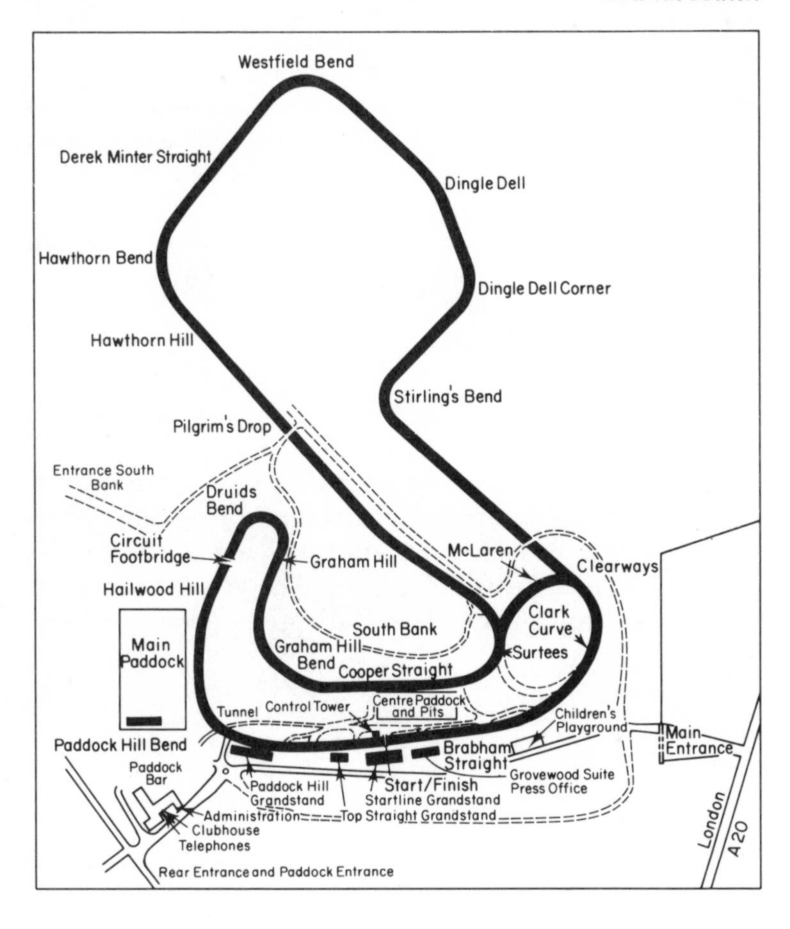
Westfield Bend
Derek Minter Straight
Dingle Dell
Hawthorn Bend
Dingle Dell Corner
Hawthorn Hill
Stirling's Bend
Pilgrim's Drop
Entrance South Bank
Druids Bend
Circuit Footbridge
Graham Hill
McLaren
Clearways
Hailwood Hill
Clark Curve
South Bank
Main Paddock
Graham Hill Bend
Surtees
Cooper Straight
Tunnel
Control Tower
Centre Paddock and Pits
Children's Playground
Paddock Hill Bend
Brabham Straight
Main Entrance
Paddock Bar
Paddock Hill Grandstand
Start/Finish
Startline Grandstand
Grovewood Suite
Press Office
Administration
Top Straight Grandstand
Clubhouse
Telephones
London
A20
Rear Entrance and Paddock Entrance

CADWELL PARK

Situation: 8 miles North of Horncastle in Lincolnshire. 134 miles from London; 30 miles from Grimsby. Approached by the A153 from Horncastle some 8 miles to the South.

Address: Cadwell Park International Racing Circuit, Louth, Lincolnshire. Telephone: Stenigot 248.

Circuit Length: 2.25 miles.

General Practice: Check by telephone.

In lovely country, Cadwell Park is the most picturesque of British Circuits. Most photographs show cars going up the Mountain, a piece of exciting track which gets cars off the ground and flying through the air. The ground is not flat but in the form of a valley which gives good spectator viewing.

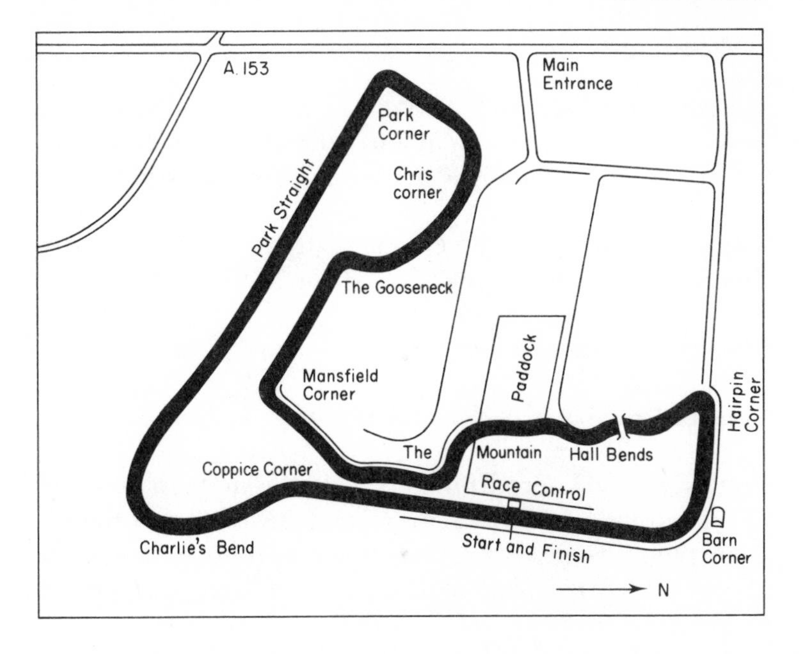
A. 153
Main Entrance
Park Corner
Chris corner
Park Straight
The Gooseneck
Paddock
Mansfield Corner
Hairpin Corner
The
Mountain
Hall Bends
Coppice Corner
Race Control
Charlie's Bend
Start and Finish
Barn Corner
N

CASTLE COOMBE

Situation: 5 miles North West of Chippenham, in Wiltshire. Approached from Chippenham on the A420, then right on to the B4099. London is 100 miles away and Bristol 19.

Address: Castle Coombe Circuit, Chippenham, Wiltshire. Telephone: Castle Coombe 782205 or 782395.

Circuit Length: 1.84 miles.

General Practice: Check by telephone.

Run over an old aerodrome, the circuit is quite flat but the meetings, although not very frequent, have a nice "Clubby" atmosphere. Basically a drivers circuit as there is really only one good corner for spectators, that they can get at properly.

Quarry Corner is about the best known as it tightens deceptively and goes on longer than drivers realise resulting in an exceptional number of spins and incidents. Camp Corner, near the Paddock, is the other favourite corner for dramas.

There are no pits, which is a little unusual, which means that if you have mechanical trouble during a race you're on your own.

While in the area a visit to the prize winning village of Castle Coombe itself is a must. It is really quite beautiful.

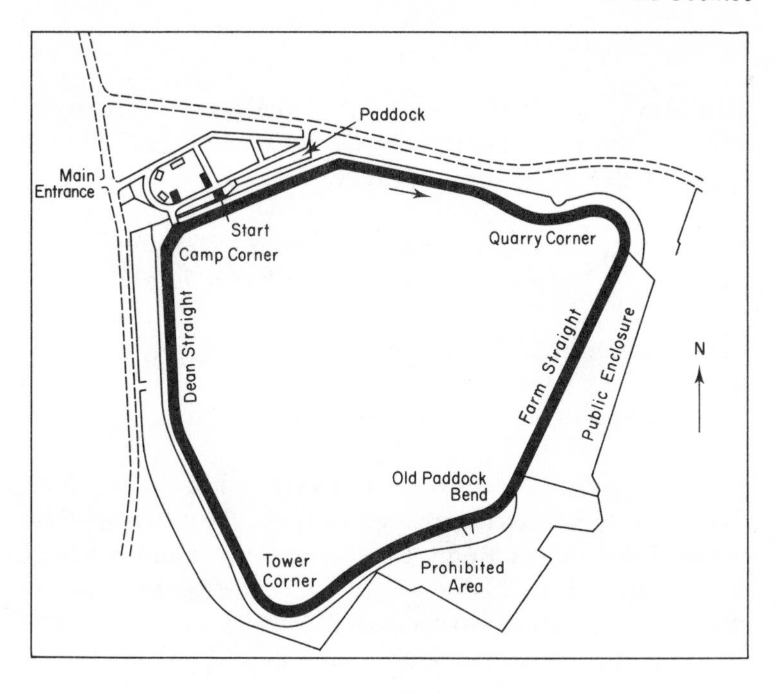
Paddock
Main
Entrance
Start
Camp Corner
Quarry Corner
Dean Straight
Farm Straight
Public Enclosure
N
Old Paddock
Bend
Tower
Corner
Prohibited
Area

CROFT AUTODROME

Situation: 5 miles south of Darlington, Durham. Approached from Darlington on A167 via Croft. Not far from A1. 238 miles from London.

Address: Croft Autodrome Ltd., Croft, Darlington, Co. Durham. Telephone: Darlington 720206 or 720659.

Circuit Length: 1.75 miles.

General Practice: Check by telephone.

A former airfield and so flat and exposed to the weather. Facilities are not luxurious. Spectating is best between the chicane and Tower Bend, though one can wander round the circuit if one chooses. The last grandstand is at the chicane. Take lots of warm clothes. Although it is a long way from London, this is a popular circuit and there are plenty of meetings, during the season.

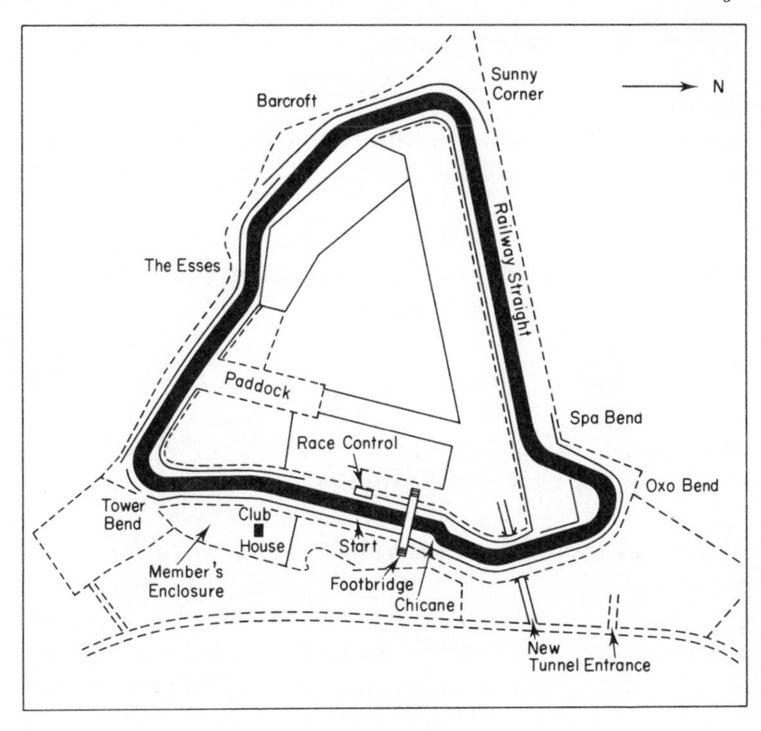

Sunny
Corner
N
Barcroft
Railway Straight
The Esses
Paddock
Spa Bend
Race Control
Oxo Bend
Tower
Bend
Club
House
Start
Member's
Enclosure
Footbridge
Chicane
New
Tunnel Entrance

INGLISTON

Situation: 7 miles west of Edinburgh on the A8 road to Glasgow, not far from Edinburgh airport. Some 37 miles from Glasgow. Regular buses from Edinburgh. 370 miles from London.

Address: Scotcircuits Ltd., National Bank Chambers, Duns, Berwickshire. Telephone: Duns 3724.

Circuit Length: 1.03 miles.

General Practice: Club practice days are organised by the Scottish Motor Club during summer months.

A short twisty circuit, with only 16 starters per race allowed, but this produces excellent racing and spectating. Good grandstands over-look the start/finish area. Usually good organisation. Good facilities, and good eating in the central pavilion. A splendid little circuit, it benefits from being part of a large showground which has its own excellent facilities and buildings.

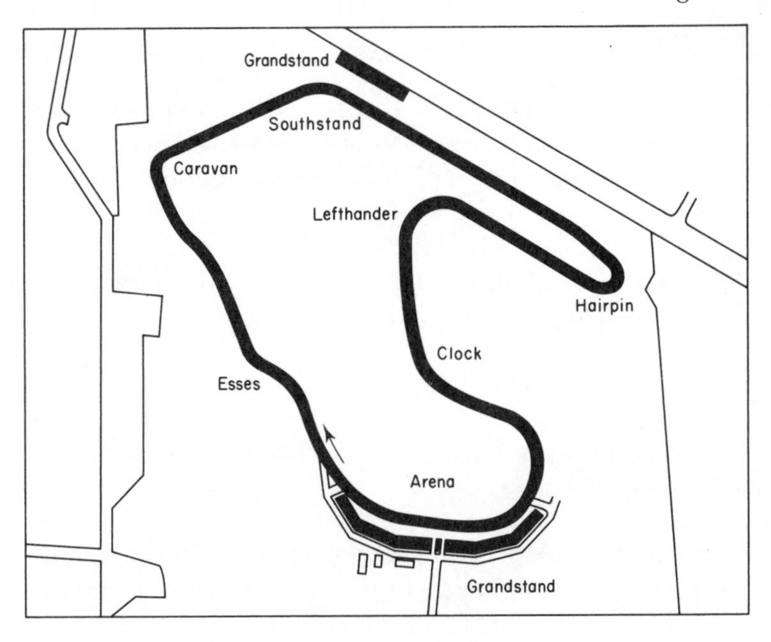
Grandstand
Southstand
Caravan
Lefthander
Hairpin
Clock
Esses
Arena
Grandstand

KNOCKHILL

Situation: 4 miles north of Dunfermline, in Fife, Scotland on the A823. This is just north of Edinburgh and across the Firth of Forth. Some 389 miles from London, 16 from Edinburgh and 39 from Glasgow.

Address: Knockhill Racing Circuit, Dunfermline, Fife. Telephone Dunfermline 23337.

Circuit Length: 1.3 miles.

General Practice: Every weekday by arrangement, and some evenings.

A new circuit which has not yet got extensive facilities, but it has good spectating being in undulating country and also has space for 1000 cars at trackside car parks, affording viewing from vehicles, a useful feature in the Scottish climate. Expected to develop fast.

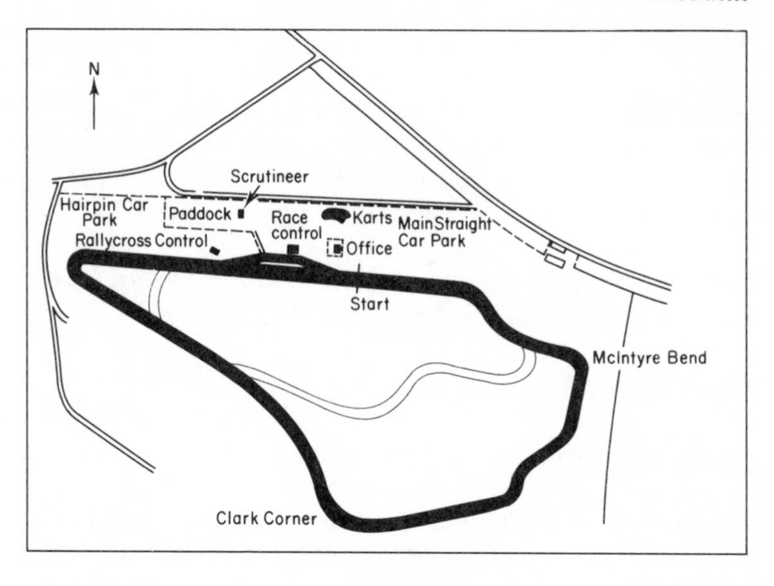
N
Scrutineer
Hairpin Car Park
Paddock
Race control
Karts
Main Straight Car Park
Rallycross Control
Office
Start
McIntyre Bend
Clark Corner

LLANDOW

Situation: 4 miles south west of Cowbridge (of where?). Cowbridge is in Wales, 13 miles west of Cardiff, and 166 miles from London. In the county of Glamorgan. A48 to Cowbridge and on to the B4270 going south-west.

Address: South Wales Automobile Club, 5 Meteor Street, Cardiff. Telephone Cardiff 27240.

Circuit Length: 1.00 miles.

General Practice: Check by telephone.

To those of us spoilt by the pleasures of Brands Hatch, this is not the most exciting circuit. A short circuit, of simple oval shape, typical ex-airfield layout and facilities. But it is the only circuit in Wales and is near the main population centres.

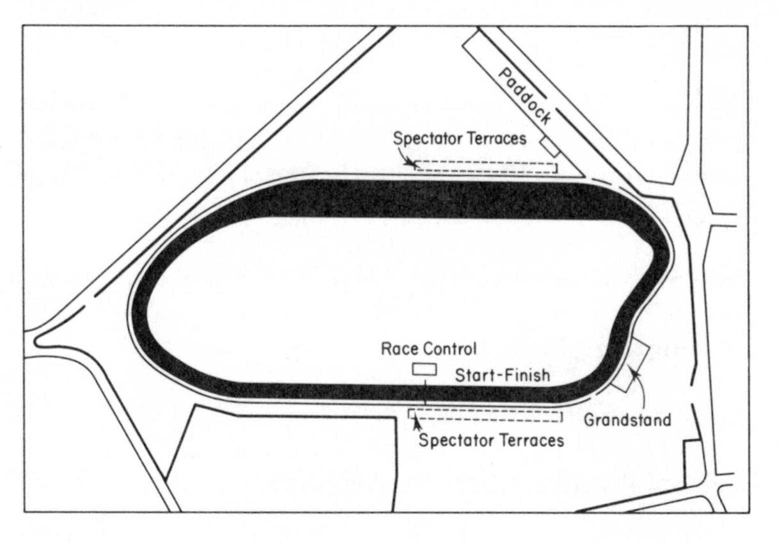
Paddock
Spectator Terraces
Race Control
Start-Finish
Grandstand
Spectator Terraces

LONGRIDGE

Situation: About 8 miles from Preston, Lancashire, on the B5269. 5 miles east of M62 junctions 31 and 32. 30 miles from Liverpool, 30 from Manchester, 17 from Blackpool and 212 from London.

Address: Lancashire Car Circuit (Longridge), Robson Way, Highfurlong, Blackpool. Telephone Blackpool 3865 or Longridge 3865.

Circuit Length: 0.43 mile.

General Practice: Check by telephone.

A most unusual circuit this, being less than ½ a mile long and only allowed a maximum number of 10 starters per race. But good fun none-the-less. It is built in a quarry with a steep side and a more gently sloping side, both of which give good viewing. No grandstands but spectating is easy and good. The lap record stands at under 25 seconds at a speed of some 65 mph, so that these 10 competitors lap at four times a minute on average, and the tightness of the circuit and slow speed leads to close, hard-fought racing. Exciting stuff. Catering and toilet facilities are simple but adequate.

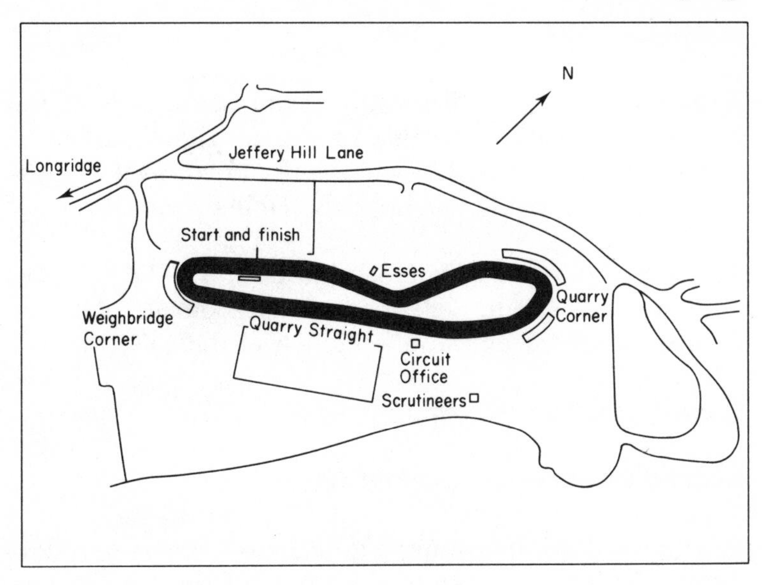
N
Jeffery Hill Lane
Longridge
Start and finish
Esses
Quarry
Corner
Weighbridge
Corner
Quarry Straight
Circuit
Office
Scrutineers

LYDDEN CIRCUIT

Situation: On A2, 7 miles south-east of Canterbury on the Dover road. Take a turning off to the right marked to Wooton/Shepherdswell. Some 2 miles north-west of Lydden village. 63 miles from London, 9 miles from Dover.

Address: William Mark Holdings Ltd., 71 West Street, Sittingbourne, Kent. Telephone Sittingbourne 72926 or 71978. Circuit telephone, Shepherdswell 830557.

Circuit Length: 1.00 mile.

General Practice: Contact Manager.

In a gentle bowl, spectating is good, and it is easy to follow the progress of cars round the whole of the circuit. The circuit is short and not very fast, but this means good racing. It is simple and undeveloped, without grandstands and only basic catering and facilities. Very much an enthusiast's circuit. Sometimes called Lydden Hill.

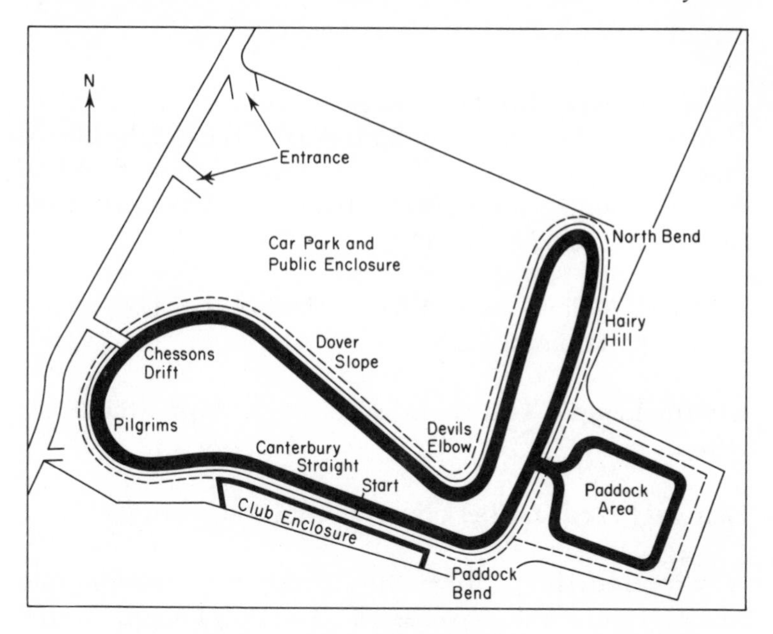
N
Entrance
Car Park and
Public Enclosure
North Bend
Hairy
Hill
Dover
Slope
Chessons
Drift
Pilgrims
Devils
Elbow
Canterbury
Straight
Start
Paddock
Area
Club Enclosure
Paddock
Bend

MALLORY PARK

Situation: Near Kirkby Mallory, just off the A47 between Hinkley and Leicester. Not far from the M1 and the M6. 31 miles from Birmingham, 8 miles from Leicester and 97 from London. From the M1 go from exit 21 to the A46 and then on the A582 to the A47.

Address: Mallory Park, Kirkby Mallory, Leicester. Telephone: Earl Shilton 42931.

Circuit Length: Full circuit 1.35 miles, short circuit 1.01 miles.

General Practice: Check by telephone.

A very pretty little circuit with a lake in the middle into which competitors have spun. The advantages of the location for spectators from the Midlands and an ability to see almost the whole circuit from almost any point, are countered by fairly uninteresting corners, except for Gerards, which for the competitors is one of those bends which never seems to end.

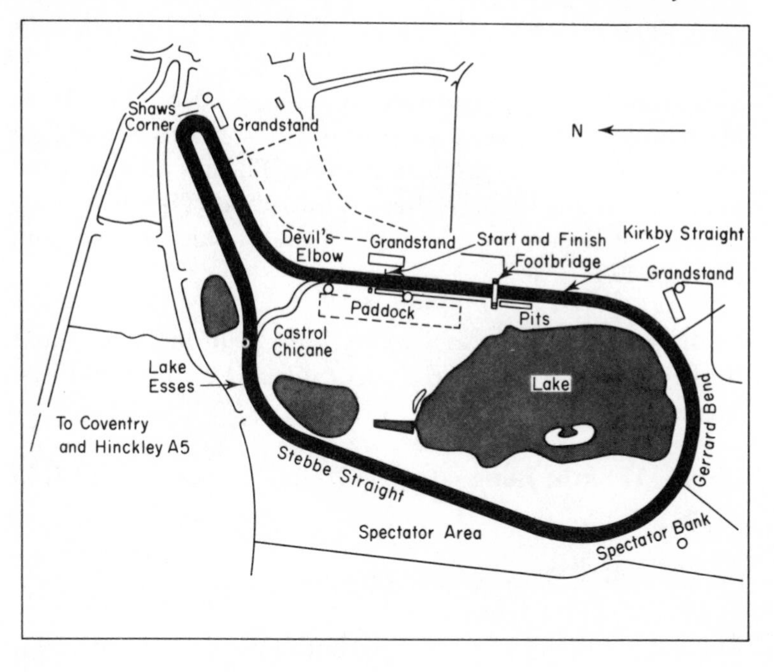
Shaws Corner
Grandstand
N
Devil's Elbow
Grandstand
Start and Finish
Kirkby Straight
Footbridge
Grandstand
Paddock
Pits
Castrol Chicane
Lake
Lake Esses
To Coventry and Hinckley A5
Gerrard Bend
Stebbe Straight
Spectator Area
Spectator Bank

OULTON PARK

Situation: Near Tarporley, Cheshire. Not far from Manchester and Liverpool, East of Chester and North East of Crewe. The M6 is just 9 miles away. The circuit is reached by main road from either Whitcombe, Northwich or Chester. Chester is 11 miles away, Liverpool 28 and London 171.

Address: Cheshire Car Circuit Ltd., Oulton Park, Little Budworth, near Tarporley, Cheshire. Telephone: Little Budworth 301.

Circuit Length: Long circuit 2.76 miles, short circuit 1.65 miles.

Practice: Special cases only, on application.

Altered, in the mid '70s, to give both long and short circuit configurations, Oulton Park is a real drivers circuit. Lodge Corner, a sharp downhill right-hander with reverse camber is perhaps the most infamous; its certainly the most spectacular. Knicker Brook, named after a courting couple disturbed by nearby blasting (honestly!) while lying in the long grass there, and Old Hall just after the pits, are two other corners which have caught out many an experienced driver, as well as newcomers.

This is a good viewing circuit for spectators although recent construction of safety fences and banks has restricted this somewhat, and there are plenty of race meetings during the year.

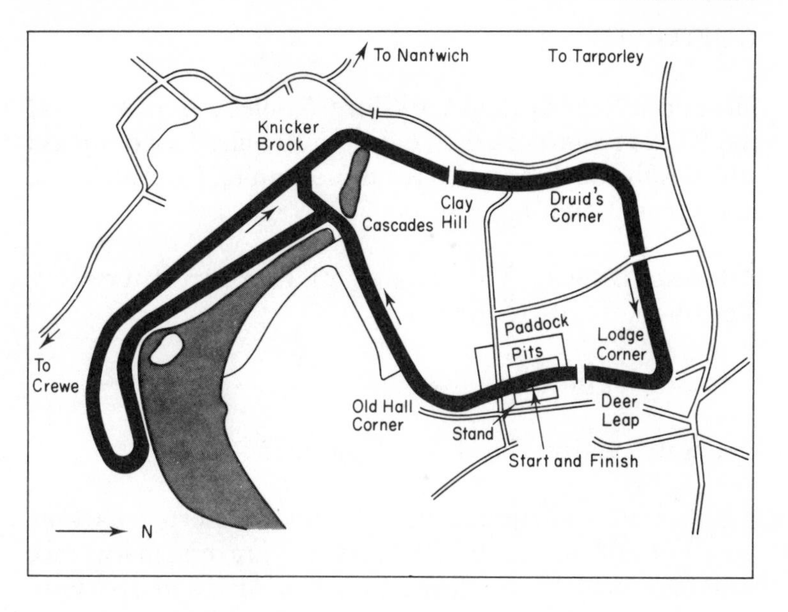
To Nantwich
To Tarporley
Knicker Brook
Clay Hill
Druid's Corner
Cascades
To Crewe
Paddock
Pits
Lodge Corner
Old Hall Corner
Stand
Deer Leap
Start and Finish
N

RUFFORTH

Situation: Near York in Yorkshire. 5 miles west of York off the B1224 from York or Wetherby. 10 miles East of the A1 which is the best approach for those coming from afar. 196 miles from London.

Address: BRSCC, York House, 21 Park Street, Leeds 1. Telephone Leeds 458659.

Circuit Length: 1.70 miles.

General Practice: Check by telephone.

Another airfield circuit, this time not a deserted wartime one, but still in use by RAF. There are not many race meetings held here. Three in 1976. Flat and spacious, spectators are allowed on the south east side only, though they can see across to the main straight. No buildings, no cover, only temporary tents and the like. No access to distant paddock. No cover in bad weather.

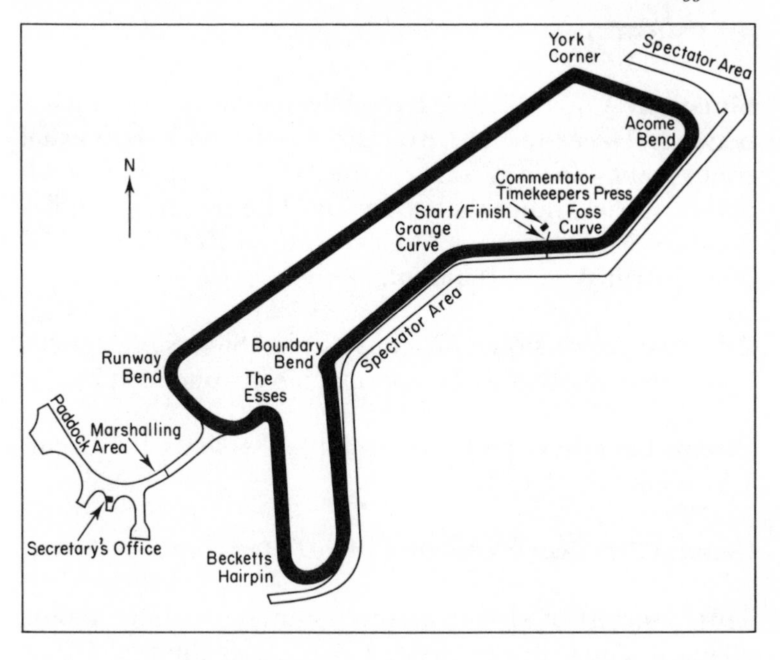
York Corner
Spectator Area
Acome Bend
N
Commentator
Timekeepers Press
Start/Finish
Grange Curve
Foss Curve
Spectator Area
Boundary Bend
Runway Bend
The Esses
Paddock
Marshalling Area
Secretary's Office
Becketts Hairpin

SILVERSTONE

Situation: A quarter-mile from Silverstone village which is between Towcester and Brackley on the A43. The usual route going North is to leave the M1 at Newport Pagnell and turn back under the motorway. The circuit is 15 miles South of Northampton, 7 miles North of Brackley and 64 miles North West of London.

Address: Silverstone Circuits Ltd., Silverstone, near Towcester, Northants. Telephone: Silverstone 857271.

Circuit Length: Grand Prix circuit 2.93 miles, Club circuit 1.61 miles.

General Practice: Frequent. Contact Manager.

This, the fastest circuit in the country, is where motor racing in Great Britain started again after the war. It has been the scene of historic wheel to wheel race long dices which have endeared it to racegoers and it has long been known as the "home of the British Grand Prix" although this now moves every second year to Brands Hatch.

Woodcote corner is one of the two most famous in the country (the other being Paddock Bend at Brands Hatch) and has long been a source of conjecture as to whether different drivers would take it "flat" or not. A chicane has now been built right on the apex which has rather taken the sting out, but it doesn't affect the Club circuit.

Silverstone is built on an old aerodrome and is quite flat except for a slight rise going up towards Maggots. Spectator viewing is quite good although the latest rebuilding of the Pits (for the second time in ten years) has made it virtually impossible to see the cars in the Paddock during big meetings. Facilities in respect of food and drink, as at other circuits, can be pretty awful so bring a hamper. Just like Snetterton it can be very cold indeed during Spring and

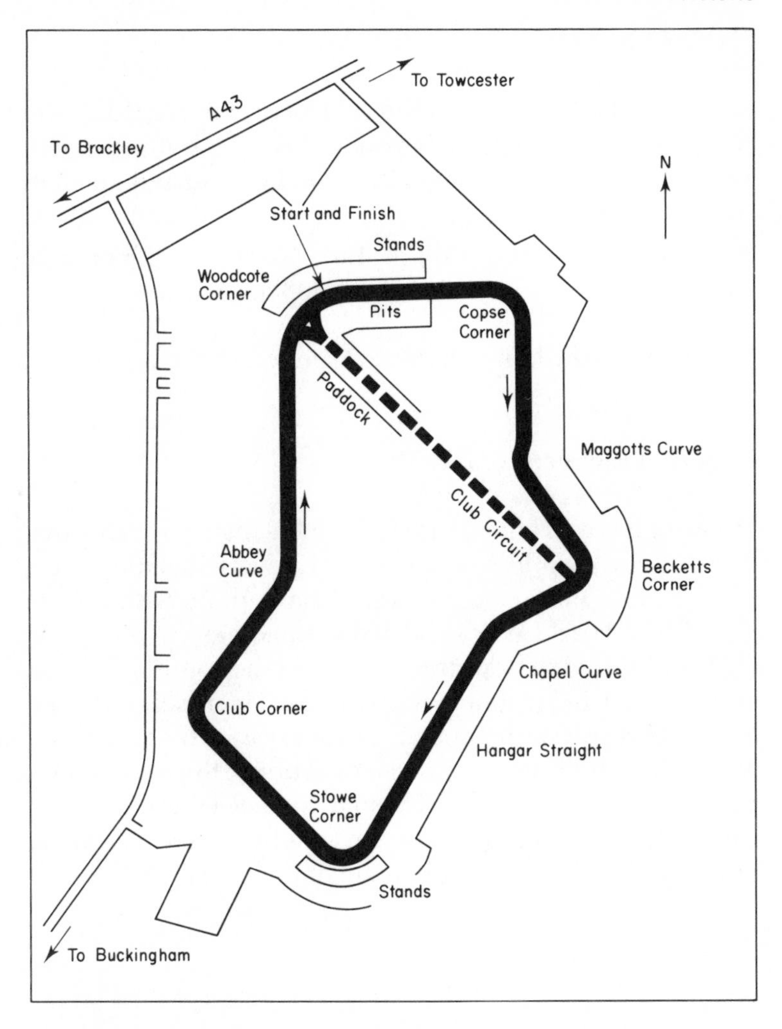

Autumn so have lots of warm clothes.

After meetings there is always a good collection of cars and enthusiasts at "the Green Man" in Syresham just down the A43 towards Brackley. This is also a good pub in which to stay, but book early.

SNETTERTON

Situation: In Norfolk, on the A11 between Thetford and Norwich, about 10 miles beyond Thetford and just South West of Attleborough. 90 miles from London and 19 miles from Norwich.
Address: Snetterton Circuit Ltd, Snetterton, Norwich, Norfolk. Telephone: Quidenham 303 or 304.

Circuit Length: Long circuit 2.71 miles, short circuit 1.92 miles.

General Practice: Contact Manager.

Home of the well known Jim Russell Racing Drivers School, this circuit is, would you believe, on a disused airfield. Just what British motor racing would have done without the R.A.F. and World War II is hard to imagine.

One of the coldest, wettest circuits in the country, it is flat and exposed and it almost always rains. The Esses or Russell are the best spectating points. The hairpin at the end of the Norwich straight sees quite a lot of action if the big circuit is being used. Sear is inaccessible and Ritchies average. Coram is long and fast and not an area for much overtaking or interest. Facilities are adequate but minimal.

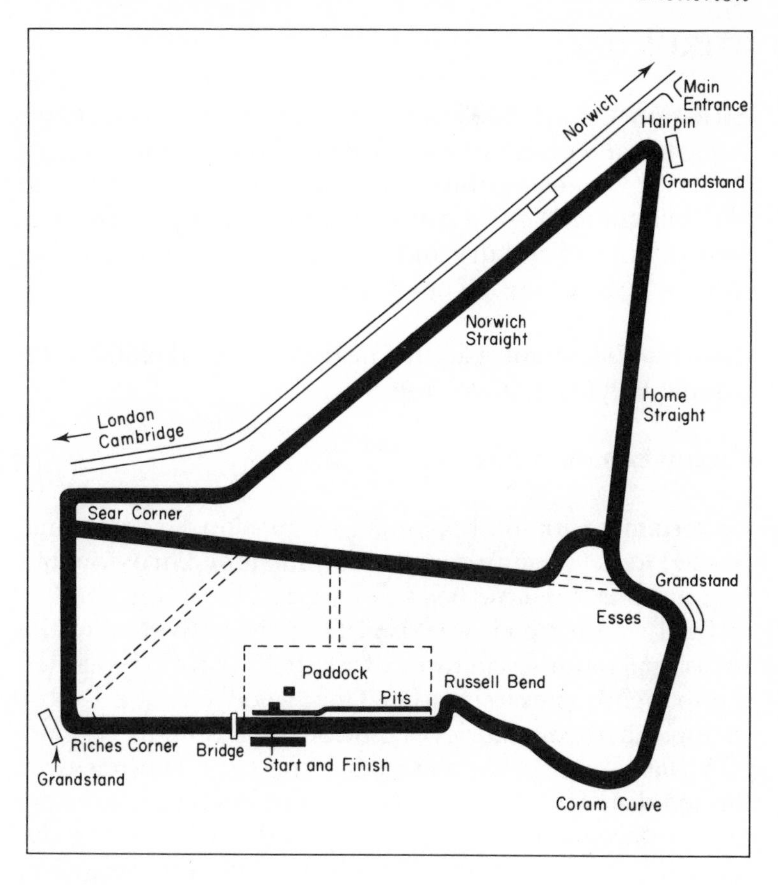

Norwich
Main Entrance
Hairpin
Grandstand
Norwich Straight
Home Straight
London
Cambridge
Sear Corner
Grandstand
Esses
Paddock
Pits
Russell Bend
Riches Corner
Bridge
Start and Finish
Grandstand
Coram Curve

THRUXTON

Situation: On the A303 which runs generally parallel to the A30, but a wee bit to the North. About 4 miles west of Andover in Hampshire on the A303 and just past Weyhill going West, it can be seen on the right. 16 miles North East of Salisbury and 70 miles West of London, but quick and easy to reach down the M3.

Address: Thruxton Circuit, near Andover, Hants. Telephone: Weyhill 2607 or 2696.

Circuit Length: 2.36 miles.

Uncertainty with local planning permission for some time has led to delays in proper development of Thruxton, but happily this has now been resolved. This is yet another airfield circuit which was used for private flying and the occasional motor cycle race before the B.A.R.C. developed it into their home circuit when Goodwood was closed to car racing. Ah, the memories of glorious Goodwood!

A flat circuit, with reasonable spectator viewing over limited distances. For drivers the most interesting corners are the three-in-one half a mile past the pits, bearing the name of former drivers Campbell, Cobb and Seagrave. Another interesting one is Club Corner before the pits where, after the long Brooklands 'straight', there is always a lot of manouvering and overtaking as cars brake for this tight left and right. Facilities are good and improving.

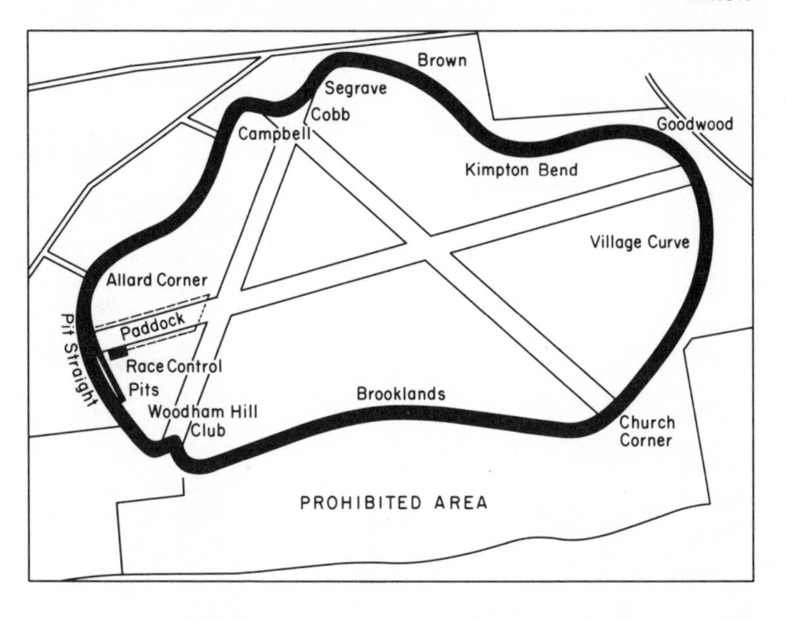

Brown
Segrave
Cobb
Campbell
Goodwood
Kimpton Bend
Village Curve
Allard Corner
Paddock
Pit Straight
Race Control
Pits
Woodham Hill
Club
Brooklands
Church
Corner
PROHIBITED AREA

Addresses

Autosport,
Haymarket Publishing Ltd.,
Regent House,
54/62 Regent Street,
London, W.1.

The weekly British motor racing "bible."

British Motor Racing Marshalls Club,
c/o L. D. Pullen,
10, Church Drive,
Harrow, Middlesex.

British Racing & Sports Car Club,
Empire House,
Chiswick High Road,
London, W.4.

British Automobile Racing Club,
Thruxton Motor Racing Circuit,
Thruxton,
Andover, Hants.

British Racing Drivers Club Ltd.,
Silverstone Racing Circuit,
Towcester, Northamptonshire.

Not until you've 'arrived.'

British Womens' Racing Drivers Club,
c/o Mrs. G. Rindlisbacher,
31, Hillersdon Avenue,
Barnes, London S.W.13.

Chater and Scott Ltd., World of Motoring Bookshop, Syon Park, Brentford, Middlesex.	Motor Racing books by post.
Civil Service Motoring Association, 797 London Road, Thornton Heath, Surrey.	Huge membership.

Classic Saloon Car Club,
7, Dunstable Road,
Caddington,
Luton, Bedfordshire.

Clubmans Register,
10, Gonnerston,
Mount Pleasant,
St. Albans, Herts.

Formula Vee Association,
Volkswagen House,
Brighton Road,
Purley, Surrey.

Historic Sports Car Club,
2/17 The Birtles,
Wythenshawe Town Centre,
Manchester.

Mini Seven Club,
Lassman Automobile Engineers Ltd.,
11/12 West Hampstead Mews,
London, N.W.6.

Monoposto Racing Club,
c/o A. J. Parsfield Esq.,
"Tonjea,"
Hilltop Manor,
Wrotham, Kent.

Motor Books and Accessories,
33, St. Martins Court,
St. Martins Lane,
London, W.C.2.

Motor racing books by post.

Motor Circuit Developments Ltd.,
Brands Hatch,
Fawkham,
near Dartford, Kent.

Motor Racing Stables,
Brands Hatch,
Fawkham,
near Dartford, Kent.

If you've never driven a single-seater racing car, go along for a trial lesson in one of the schools Formula Fords.

Motoring News,
Standard House,
Bonhill Street,
London, E.C.2.

The weekly motor sport newspaper.

Royal Automoble Club,
Motor Sport Division,
31, Belgrave Square,
London, S.W.1.

British motor sports administration headquarters.

Scottish Motor Racing Club Ltd.,
National Bank Chambers,
Duns, Berwickshire,
Scotland.

Royal Irish Automoble Club, 34, Dawson Street, Dublin 2, Ireland.	Try a motor racing week-end in Ireland.
Jim Russell Racing Drivers School, c/o Snetterton Circuit, near Norwich, Norfolk.	The longest established school in the country. Branches also at Mallory Park and Silverstone.
Seven-Fifty Motor Club Ltd., c/o D. Bradley Esq., "Zolder", 16 Woodstock Road, Witney, Oxfordshire.	
Steering Wheel Club, 47, Curzon Street, London, W.1.	Quiet, peaceful and nostalgic. An excellent spot to give your sponsor lunch. Members only.
Veteran Car Club of Great Britain, 14 Fitzhardinge Street, London, W.1.	
Vintage Sports Car Club, 121 Russell Road, Newbury, Berkshire.	No test drives. They just look for serious would-be racing drivers.
Winfield Racing Drivers School, Goodwood Circuit, near Chichester, Sussex.	

Specialised Racing Car Manufacturers

This list is not necessarily complete nor is it necessarily totally correct; it should be used merely as a guide. Sadly, in the modern highly commercial world of motor racing, even at Club level, many small manufacturers who start out with good intentions often find that in their search for perfection in their cars, they lose sight of the necessity to be properly capitalised and to show at least a token profit. Thus, after an eager and enthusiastic start, they find it impossible to combine the attributes of designer, manufacturer, tester and salesman under one roof and either return to racing a proprietory car themselves, or leave racing altogether.

Therefore, before buying a new car, make sure that there will be an adequate supply of spares and parts from the parent factory for as long as you intend to keep it and remember that if the factory should have the missfortune to go out of business, the re-sale value of your car will drop.

Alexis Cars Ltd., Halloughton Grange, Whitacre, Coleshill, Birmingham.	Formula 3 Formula Ford Formula Super Vee
Chevron Cars, Derek Bennet Engineering Ltd., 105 Chorley Old Road, Bolton, Lancs.	Formula 3
Crossle Car Company Ltd., Rory's Wood, Knockagoney, Co. Down, North Ireland.	Formula Ford
Colchester Racing Developments Ltd., Little Bentley, Colchester, Essex.	Formula Ford

Dastle Manufacturing Company, Tythebarns Lane, Send, Woking, Surrey.	Formula Ford Formula 3
Delta Racing Cars Ltd., Unit 3, Wrecclesham Trading Estate, Farnham, Surrey.	Formula 4
Elden International Racing Ltd., Tower Garage, Wrotham Hill, Wrotham, Kent.	Formula Ford Formula Super Vee
FSL Cars Ltd., Newcroft Estate, Tangmere, Chichester, Sussex.	Formula Ford
Chris Greville-Smith, 127, Sir Henry Parkes Road, Canley, Coventry.	Clubmans
Ginetta Cars Ltd., West End Motor Works. Witham Essex.	Sports G.T.
Hawke Racing Cars Ltd., Municipal Airport, Southend-on-Sea, Essex.	Formula Ford
Jamun Racing, Eastern House, Court Lodge, Bush Road, Cuxton, Rochester, Kent.	Formula Ford

Lola Cars Ltd., Glebe Road, St. Peters Road, Huntingdon, Cambridgeshire.	Formula Super Vee
Maxperenco Products Ltd., Lower Broadway, Didcot, Oxfordshire.	Formula Ford
Mallock Racing, Mill Cottage, The Grove, Roade, Northampton.	Clubmans
March Cars Ltd., Murdock Road, Bicester, Oxfordshire.	Formula 3
MRE (Racing Services) Ltd., 1, Station Road, Bourne End, Buckinghamshire.	Formula Ford
Mini-Jem, Salthouse Mills, Salthouse, Barrow-in-Furness, Cumbria.	Sports cars
Modus Cars Ltd., Unit 11, Watton Industries Centre, Norwich Road, Watton, Norfolk.	Formula 3 Formula Super Vee
Nicholls Engineering and Development Ltd., 35, Meddon Street, Bideford, North Devon.	Clubmans Formula Ford Formula 3

Pallister Racing Cars, 11, Upland Mews, Upland Road, London, S.E.22.	Formula 3 Formula Ford
Ron Taurenac Racing Ltd., Sneglar Road, Woking, Surrey.	Formula 3
Ray Race, 65, North Street, Clapham, London, S.W.4.	Formula 3 Formula Ford
Royale Racing Ltd., Unit 70, Little Staughton Airfield, Little Staughton, near Bedford.	Formula Ford Formula Super Vee
Safir Engineering Ltd., 1, Cleveland Close, Walton-on-Thames, Surrey.	Formula 3
Tiga, Tim Schenken-Howden Ganley Ltd., 361, Bath Road, Chippenham, Slough, Bucks.	Formula Ford
Titan Cars Ltd., The Harley Works, Paxton Hill, St. Neots, Cambs	Formula Ford
Van Diemen International Racing Services, Chalk Road, Snetterton, Norwich, Norfolk.	Formula Ford Formula 3

Competition Component and Product Manufacturers and Suppliers

Brake Manufacturers

Automotive Products,
Tachbrook Road,
Lemington Spa,
Warwicks.
0926 27000

Girling,
Birmingham Road, West Bromwich, West Midlands.
021–553 2969
(also suspension component manufacturer.)

Competition Brake Pads and Linings

Ferodo Competitions Department,
Chapel-en-le-Frith,
near Stockport, Cheshire SK12 6JP.
0298–81 2520.

Mintex,
P.O. Box 18, Cleckheaton,
West Yorkshire BD19 3UJ.
097–62 2535.

Carburettor Parts Suppliers

S.U.,
Wood Lane, Erdington,
Birmingham B24 9QS.
021–373 7371.

Weber,
Fiat (England) Limited,
Great West Road,
Brentford, Middx. TW8 9DJ.
01–568 8822.

Zenith, Solex & Stromberg,
Honeypot Lane, Stanmore,
Middx. HA7 1EG.
01–204 3388.

Electrical Component Manufacturer and Auxiliary Light Suppliers

Bosch,
Rhodes Way, Radlett Road,
Watford, Herts. WD2 4UB.
0923 44233.

Luscas (Sales and Service Division—also Competitions Section),
Great Hampton Street,
Birmingham B18 6AU.
021–236 5050.

Wipac of Buckingham,
Buckingham MK18 1BH.
028–02 3031.

Lighting

Carello, Lyall Lusted
Limited,
Vincent Works,
Vincent Lane, Dorking,
Surrey RH4 3HJ.
0306 4091/2.

Cibie, Britover
(Continental) Limited,
387/389 Chapter Road,
London NW2 5HG.
01–459 7256.

Hella,
Daventry Road Industrial
Estate, Banbury, Oxen
OX16 7JU.
0295 56381.

Marchal,
Great West Road,
Brentford, Middx. TW8
94P.
01–560 2111
(also Trico screen-wiping and washing equipment.)

Instruments

Smiths Industries, Motor
Accessory Division,
Cricklewood Works,
Cricklewood, London NW2
6NN.
01–452 5337.

Helmets

Griffon Helmets,
Highfield Road, Cradley,
near Halesowen, West
Midlands B63 2DH.
Cradley Heath
64343/64780/64190.

Restall,
Anne Road, Smethwick,
Warley, West Midlands
B66 2NZ.
021–558 4761/3.

Oil Companies

Castrol,
Burmah House, Pipers
Way, Swindon, Wiltshire
SN3 1RE.
0793 30151.

Duckhams,
Summit House, Glebe Way,
West Wickham, Kent BR4
0SJ.
01–777 0600.

Esso (Motor Sport
Division),
Esso House, 94–8 Victoria
Street, London SW1E 5JW.
01–834 6677.

Shellsport,
P.O. Box 148, Shell,
Strand, London WC2R
0DX.
01–438 276.

Texaco,
1 Knightsbridge Green,
London SW1X 7QJ.
01–584 5000.

Total,
33 Cavendish Square,
London W1M 0JE.
01–449 6393.

Special Steering Wheels

Astrali,
Redhouse Industrial
Estate, Anglian Road,
Aldridge, Staffordshire
WS9 8EP.
0922–54815.

Sumpguards

Magard,
Duplex Works, Fernie
Road, Market Harborough,
Leicestershire LE16 7PH.
0645 7041.
(also manufacturers of Minilite magnesium and light alloy wheels.)

Tech-Del,
32–6 Telford Way, Brunel
Road, Acton, London W3
7XD.
01–743 0103.

Suspension Component and Shock Absorber Manufacturers

Armstrong,
Gibson Lane, Melton,
North Ferriby, North
Humbershire HU14 3HY.
Hull (0482) 633311.

Woodhead,
Moorcroft Works, Ossett,
West Yorkshire.
092–43 3521.

Shock Absorbers

Konis,
J.W.E. Banks & Sons
Limited,
St. Guthlac's Lodge,
Crowland, near
Peterborough PE6 0JP.
073–17 316.

Spax,
61 Fortess Road, London
NW5 1AD.
01–485 6721.

Tyres

Avon,
Melksham, Wiltshire.
022–16 3911.

Dunlop Competitions
Department,
Fort Dunlop, Birmingham
B24 9QT.
021–373 2121.

Goodyear Competitions
Department,
Bushbury, Wolverhampton
WV10 6DH.
0902 22321.

Kleber Competitions
Department,
Pump Lane, Hayes, Middx.
01–848 3451.

Tuning and Accessory Shops

Auto Equipe,
63 Queens Road, Hastings,
Sussex.
Hastings 430494.

Checkpoint Race and Rally
Equipment,
1 Northfield Industrial
Estate, Beresford Avenue,
Wembley, Middx. HA0
1XF.
01–903 0111.

City Speed Centre,
58 Kingsholm Road,
Gloucester,
Gloucestershire.
Gloucester 20784.

Demon Tweeks,
Gateshead Smithey,
Tattenhall, near Chester,
Cheshire.
0829 70625/70055.

Derrington,
159 London Road,
Kingston, Surrey.
01–546 5621.

G.P. Speed Equipment,
Royal Parade, Chislehurst,
Kent.
01–467 3160.

Charles Jenkins and Sons,
New Road, Pengham,
Glamorgan, South Wales.
0443 832044.

Chris Montague
Carburettor Company,
380/2 Finchley Road,
London NW2 2HP.
01–794 7766/7.

Kerr's Kar Parts,
568 Foleshill Road,
Coventry, Warwickshire.
Coventry 87932.

Larkspeed,
12 Station Road,
Crossgates, Leeds 15,
Yorkshire.
0532 606330.

Leedspeed,
7 Crookes Road, Sheffield
S10 5BA, Yorkshire.
0742 661779.

Les Leston,
315 Finchley Road,
London NW3 6EH.
01–435 5665.

Mini Sport
7 Church Street, Padiham,
Lancashire.
Padiham 73285 and 73620.

Mitcham Motors,
472 London Road,
Mitcham, Surrey.
01–648 3865.

Motocare,
235 Deansgate, Manchester
M3 4EN.
061–832 8230.

Motorspeed & Sports-Tune
(Accessories),
10 Brandon Terrace,
Edinburgh. Waverley
(Edinburgh) 3507 and
98 Paisley Road West,
Glasgow.
041–427 2306.

Ralley Equipe,
90 Croston's Road, Bury,
Lancashire.
061–761 1178.

J & D Ralleyhouse,323
Goswell Road, Islington,
London EC1.
01–837 7250.

Ripspeed Racing,
533 Hertford Road,
Enfield, Middx. EN3 5UA.
01–804 0425.

Road and Racing
Accessories (Holborn) Ltd,
10–12 Proctor Street,
London WC1V 6NX.
01–242 3080.

Speedspares (Burnely),
74 Colne Road, Burnley,
Lancashire.
Burnley 22270.

Ton Tyre Auto,
43–50 Quarry Hill,
Tonbridge.
073–22 63333.

Index

Index